Speculations on Postcapitalism

How Digitalization Is Disrupting Everything We Know About Modern Civilization

by Anthony Signorelli

ISBN-13: 978-1719264198

Published by Blue Harbor
559 Humboldt Avenue
Saint Paul, Minnesota 55107
651-340-2196

Blue Harbor is an imprint of Signorelli Consulting Group, Inc.

Print copies are available at Amazon's Create Space: https://www.createspace.com/6910922

Cover and title design by Steve Bivans.

Works by Anthony Signorelli

On Postcapitalism
The Postcapitalism Manifesto
Speculations on Postcapitalism (print version)

For Hungry Minds…
Subscribe to **Intertwine: Mind * Heart * World**. Immediate access to blog posts, poems, tools, and special offers. Click here to sign up!
Don't miss out!

More Nonfiction
Call to Liberty: Bridging the Divide Between Liberals and Conservatives, 2006, Scarletta Press
Rooster Crows at Light from the Bombing: Poems and Essays on the Gulf War, (ed. with Paul MacAdam), 1993, Inroads Press

Table of Contents

Introduction

Digitalization is undermining capitalism, and as it does so, a lot is going to change—the problem is, we don't know exactly what those changes will be because they have not yet occurred. That's precisely why I call these essays "Speculations." I wrote them to speculate, to follow the logic, to see where it might go.

As it turns out, the possibilities are astonishing. As I will explain, the expansion of digitalization into nearly everything undermines the most basic assumptions of life on earth that we, who live in a capitalist society, hold. The central thesis is that the changes ahead are on a par with the transition from feudalism to capitalism, except that we are going from capitalism to a *postcapitalist era*. Because of this thesis, the essays collected here are wide ranging. They explore economics, politics, business, religion, climate change, and more. Many of them only provide highlights of much deeper arguments I am making in additional books on postcapitalism. I am, in fact, working on a four book series that will address the challenges, the opportunities, and new ways of thinking that will characterize this postcapitalist era.

I need to make one thing very clear: Although I believe that this move to postcapitalism is inevitable and presents an opportunity to create a new world, I do not approach this work as an advocate of postcapitalism. The postcapitalist era is going to happen. Capitalism will not be able to continue under circumstances in which, as we will see, markets malfunction. There is no need for an anti-capitalist movement. There are no laws to champion, no candidates to elect. But that doesn't mean there is nothing to do.

The outcome emanating from the digitalized postcapitalist disruption will be shaped by these forces: the implicit metaphors of the digitalized world, the intrinsic logic of that world, and the complementary ideas that define the societal conversation around postcapitalism. We have the opportunity to define a new common sense, a new set of accepted assumptions about how the world works, and the nature of the conversation we are going to have. Involvement in that conversation—yours, mine, and everyone's—is the only position I strongly advocate. What is necessary isn't a set of policy considerations; it is thought, ideas, and themes. We need people who care enough to think, write, and talk. We need you.

So, let that be both my invitation and my introduction. I hope you will enter these pages with the same curiosity and fire that got me to write them. I hope you will find them stimulating. And I hope you will join us at www.postcapfuture.com to make sure you know when the new books in the series come out, and join the conversation.

--Anthony Signorelli, August, 2017

I

Capitalism's Crisis

POSTCAPITALISM CANNOT BE CONSIDERED, MUCH LESS understood, without a comprehensive view of the existential crisis capitalism faces. The thesis of capitalism's demise always faces certain tough questions—isn't this just another incremental change? What about the real economy? Won't capitalism simply morph to meet the needs in the new world? How big a deal is this change anyway? The following essays address these and other common questions. In doing so, they create the basis for exploring the impact of this coming crisis, as well as the plan for the future.

The Coming Collapse of Capitalism

Over the next one hundred years, capitalism will come to an end. It will do so not because of a competitive system, but because its own internal logic will cause its end and require a different system to arise. In fact, two recent books make this case rather cogently—Naomi Klein's *This Changes Everything: Capitalism vs. the Climate,* and Paul Mason's *Postcapitalism: A Guide to Our Future.* Klein's book argues that climate change reveals the approaching endgame to capitalism's program of externalizing and socializing anything it cannot sell at market, climate change proves it, and even the deniers know it—that's why they deny climate change is real.[1] Mason takes a different approach. He argues that digitalization is causing markets to falter and profits to collapse. Unlike previous eras in which capitalism simply expanded into new markets, Mason argues that such traditional answers are no longer available. We'll see why in a minute.[2] My argument is not that we need to fight capitalistic powers, as Klein argues, nor is it that some new or revised brand of socialism will be the inevitable replacement for capitalism, as Mason eventually argues. The true power of both writers is in the insight that capitalism is nearing its end because the conditions for its success no longer exist.

To understand the causes of this demise, we must understand the four key assumptions that form the foundation of capitalism's ability to sustain itself. At the birth of capitalism and through the centuries of its success, these assumptions held true. They constituted the foundation on which the capitalist system could be built and they supported and renewed capitalism in its own terms; without them, it would never have succeeded. While these assumptions have constituted capitalism's foundation for centuries, they are now crumbling as capitalism confronts its own inherent, internal contradictions.

What are those assumptions? The four assumptions are as follows:

- Markets effectively and efficiently set prices due to the opposing forces of supply and demand.

- When necessary (usually because prices and profits are trending downward) capitalism can be revitalized by discovering or creating new markets.
- Externalities remain economically external and irrelevant.
- Private property and the rule of law are sacrosanct.

These assumptions sustain capitalism so long as they hold true, and they are critical for making the capitalist economic formula work. Capitalism only works for those things that are subject to market pricing. Its inherent structure means that production costs for innovative products will always start high and trend down, and as they do, new markets must be accessed so that innovations will be highly valued again and profits renewed. At the same time, certain costs must be ignored for the formula to work, especially if those costs cannot be made subject to market pricing mechanisms. The colossal environmental, social, and human costs of externalities are simply not calculated in order to make the books balance. And finally, privatization is essential to ensure market subjection. In the early centuries, rule of law was used to enclose the commons; today, it is used to create ownership of ideas, genes, and processes so as to expand capitalism's reach. Were any one of these assumptions to fail, the system could not hold together.

And yet, in these waning days of the capitalist period, all four assumptions are beginning to fail. Markets are losing their ability to price goods and services; new markets are scarce; externalities can no longer be avoided; and private property is gradually giving way to a collaborative commons. These changes are not the result of an external threat, but rather of the natural, inevitable outcome of capitalism following its own necessary, inevitable development.

The two forces driving the failure of capitalist assumptions are globalization and digitalization. Both are inextricably linked, but we will consider them separately to illustrate how they operate. Then, we will explore the growing decay of the four assumptions and what that decay means.

Globalized Capitalism

Capitalism could not help but go global. It is always expanding and has been ever since its inception. Capitalism originated in 16th century England, and developed further with Adam Smith and the Industrial Revolution in the 18th century, but its core principles, including private property and rule of law, predate the origins by at least a century. Both ideas contributed to the erosion of feudalism—private property replaced the rights of nobility, and rule of law destroyed the political and religious power of nobility. As feudalism fell, capitalism created markets, then expanded into new markets, and continues expanding to this day. While expansion appears necessary for capitalism to survive, *why* is it necessary to survive?

It is inherent in capitalism that pricing power, and therefore the ability to generate profit, decays over time. Products are invented that are unique— they are introduced to a new market where they are unique—and therefore of high value. Over time, those same products are increasingly produced at higher productivity and with increasing efficiency. As that occurs, two outcomes can be expected: first, the marginal cost of production decreases. Capitalists love this because if they can maintain the perceived value while production costs decrease, profits grow dramatically.

Second, with increasing profits, capitalists produce more and more until the product becomes ubiquitous, loses its novelty, and prices begin to decline. Supply outstrips demand, competitors enter the market and produce even more, and prices decline toward the marginal cost of production—that is, toward the unit cost of producing one more widget. In business terms, the product becomes commoditized and profit margins shrink.

For centuries, capitalism's response to this inherent logic has been to find or create new markets using three different methods.

- First, when a capitalist nation colonizes a place, it can control the market there. Call this market expansion by conquest.
- Second, distribution systems, trade, and transportation of goods enabled a capitalist nation to serve markets that are not being served.
- Third, capitalists develop a new market by creating demand, largely through advertising and mass media, but also by innovation.

Capitalism grew new markets across the globe; it also grew deeply into nations, communities, and individual lives. Yet just as capitalism has infiltrated everywhere, it is running up against global limitations. With the expansion of capitalism since the fall of the Berlin wall in 1989, there is almost nowhere on earth that capitalism is not the dominant economic force. Geographically speaking, there are no new markets to penetrate. As pricing power gives way to commoditization, corporate leaders can no longer look to expand into new geographies because there aren't any. Capitalism is everywhere already, and every place is already a market.[i]

Likewise, business has reduced the cost of transportation of goods and services, thereby creating a nearly true global market. Digital goods and services in particular—including monetized capital—may now be transported around the globe in no time and at zero cost. But most other goods can also be transported and delivered at little or no cost to almost anywhere, and those costs are coming down. In other words, the idea of underserved markets is essentially disappearing—everyone has service everywhere, or will have it, as capitalism continues infiltrating every corner of the globe.

When conquest and colonization became less effective, capitalists turned to the third method, mass media, to create new markets. In the 20th century especially, mass media created widely accepted social "norms" that people believed they should meet. Whether for personal or business use, the new need created new demand. Innovative new products also created new needs, which accounts for the relentless drive of capitalism to create new products. In an era when big cities had one or two newspapers, three TV channels, several AM radio stations, FM only played music, and no one ever heard of the internet, everyone was watching, reading, or listening to the same thing, so a few well-placed ads could swing an entire market to perceive differently. That perception created demand—in essence, a new market.

But in today's world of hundreds of TV channels, unlimited digital radio, infinite websites and blogs, and an untold number of communities of interest organized through the internet, the ability of capitalism to efficiently create a mass market has waned. Social media still demonstrates that perceptions can be changed, but not in a cost-efficient manner from the capitalist perception. After all, *social* means relationships, not mass media. And building markets one relationship at a time is a costly proposition.

Finally, there is innovation—the creation of new products or services that generate new demand for things people don't know they need. For hundreds of years, such innovation has driven the capitalistic economy, and it still does

---

[i] This drive to new markets is what drove imperialism and colonization during the capitalist era. Mature capitalist economies largely abandoned this strategy in recent decades, but new participants, notably Russia and China, still use this approach. It will soon appear as futile to them as it does to most capitalist nations. Developed capitalist economies discovered that free trade agreements were even more effective at finding and opening new markets.

today. Large, consumer-driven businesses generally derive 80 percent of sales and profits from products invented in the preceding three to five years. In some businesses, the obsolescence cycle is so short that their profits come from products released only within the previous six months.

Capitalism has sustained itself by expanding into new markets when pricing and profits decline. It has always done so, and it has always used all four methods to accomplish its goal. But today, *there are no new markets to expand into*. Globalism means capitalism is everywhere. The disintegration of mass media gives it no effective power to create mass markets. While digital innovation can produce demand, it cannot create a functioning market. Capitalism relies on new markets and there is no way to create them anymore.

The End of Externalities

Just as capitalism stayed lively by expanding constantly into new markets over the centuries, it has maintained its power and profit by steadfastly refusing to account for externalities. The classic example of externality is pollution from a smokestack or effluent pipe that dumps into a river. When smoke goes into the air or poison into a river, capitalism has no method to account for that, so it is treated as an "externality," or a kind of unfortunate, unintended consequence. There is no cost to the factory owner—hence no accounting for it. The result included the infamous days in London in 1952 when people couldn't see in front of themselves because of the smoke and smog, the photos of Pittsburgh during the heyday of its steel mills in the 19th century, or the Cuyahoga River that actually caught fire in 1969.

Pollution is one such externality, but others include socializing risk, as we do every time there is a taxpayer bail out of the economy, and risk to health and safety of workers or consumers. Socialized risk and health and safety concerns do not show up on the financial statements of capitalist actors by design. Capitalism could not succeed if it had to account for them, so it created a system that pretends they don't exist.

When the externalities became noxious enough, people required government to do something about it, and regulation of industries is primarily driven to confront these externalities. The economic issue, however, is never resolved—it is simply turned into a political issue in which laws and regulations are imposed on capitalism to try to force proper accounting, or removed to force people to accept the risks.

Ideological capitalists argue that the issues of externalities can all be sorted out by the market. This ideological position, however, is a deception—externalities, by definition, are external; they are not in the system and the market system cannot account for them. The ideology pretends that an externality can be solved via the market, when it cannot. An actual accounting for externalities will either be ineffective or it will destroy the system itself.

One example of a famous contrived market is the cap-and-trade schemes claimed to be solutions to the atmospheric carbon problem that is driving climate change. Set a cap and grant permits to polluters, and the market will price those permits according to demand. Increased costs will force producers to limit their production—or so the theory goes. As Naomi Klein documents, the 2009 economic crisis drove down economic activity. Since there was so little economic activity, fossil fuel burning declined, and everyone wanted to unload their carbon credits. Guess what happened to the market? The bottom fell out on carbon permits. Suddenly, there was almost zero cost to emitting carbon, so there was no incentive to eliminate emissions—exactly the wrong incentive.[3] A similar market, the UN Clean Development Mechanism, underwent a similar collapse. "Weak emissions targets and the economic downturn in wealthy nations resulted in a 99 percent decline in carbon prices between 2008 and 2013," according to Oscar Reyes from the Institute for Policy Studies.[4] The volatility of carbon markets destabilizes solar and wind markets, where long term investment and consistency are required for success.

Here's the deal for capitalism: the game is up. Externalities are no longer external. The impacts can no longer be escaped by class or power. The great leveler is global climate change.

Climate change shows two inescapable truths: first, scale matters, and second, externalities will force an accounting. The globalization of capitalism has moved the externalized impact of capitalism from local centers of production to a global phenomenon. Production is everywhere, everyone is part of a market, and the externalities affect everyone. We are operating a global economic system to serve numbers of people completely unprecedented, and the impact of that activity is also affecting everyone and everything. Instead of the famous localized images of black London or steel mill Pittsburgh, we can imagine a darkening earth where the entire globe is ensconced in grey smog. Think of the images of earth from space. Gone is the beautiful blue of the oceans. Gone is the green of the continents. Gone even is the white of the moving cloud formations. All is gray. As these externalities go global, we are on the verge of stopping capitalism in its tracks, most likely through catastrophic events tied to climate change.

Markets Aren't Working Because of Digitalization

Capitalism's logic calls for it to create or expand into new markets, as we have seen, and innovation is a big part of that expansion. Since the 1980s, most of the new innovation has gone into the digital economy—information, knowledge, data, data manipulation, collection, and reporting. We have created digital systems, digital products, and digital features in non-digital products. Digitalization enables robots to take over work, and we can print objects directly from their digital plans. All of this is amazing—it is the natural output of capitalism, and it is highly problematic for capitalism.

The challenge to capitalism derives from a unique quality of digital products—they can be reproduced at zero marginal cost. Consider the digital song. An artist makes and records the music, which is saved and recorded in digital form. There is substantial cost in creating that digital code, and the artist would hope to get a return on it by selling a certain number to cover the cost, and then more to make a profit.

In the days of vinyl LPs, the musical recording was purchased in a store after having been manufactured, fitted with a cover, and shipped to the store. All those activities created cost on a per-album basis, and the total of those costs is what economists would call the marginal cost of production. In theory, the marginal cost of production creates a floor in the selling price of the product. Efficiencies and productivity may help reduce costs to make it more profitable, but there will always be competitors to drive the price toward that floor.

The old scenario works because *there is a floor below which prices cannot go,* and in such an environment, markets function effectively to set prices through supply and demand. Supply is constrained by the marginal cost of production. Demand may be bigger or smaller, and the ratio sets the price at any given point in time. Properly operating markets calibrate demand and supply through the pricing mechanism.

Here's the problem for capitalism: with digital products, markets can no longer work. Supply is infinite and the marginal cost of reproduction is zero.

Music can sit on a server somewhere and be downloaded with no cost of transportation, no cost for packaging, and no cost for producing a product. It doesn't matter if customers download one or one million copies—there is no change in cost. There is still the investment to create the product, but there is no marginal cost to reproduce. In other words, cost is zero while supply is infinite, so the supply side of the supply/demand ratio cannot be calculated. Hence, markets can no longer price things, and markets can no longer function. Prices collapse. Without markets and prices, capitalism cannot operate.[ii]

It is one thing to imagine this problem for a category like music or books; it is entirely different to realize that *everything* is becoming digitalized. Before long, most consumer products will be 3D printed at home according to a *digital* plan. Assembly lines operated by robots will put together 3D printed parts. Artificial intelligence will analyze the world and write reports, drive our cars, and administer government services. As this happens, the logic of capitalism will no longer operate, and that will lead us to a whole new world.

The Decay of Private Property

Finally, perhaps the single most stalwart principle that holds capitalism together is the principle of private property. Private property creates the notion of ownership, which is central to the notion of capital itself. Only when you have private property can a capitalist own the means of production, including land, buildings, and equipment. In a capitalist society, government establishes laws and rules for protecting and trading privately owned capital. You could say it is in the DNA of capitalist economic and political structures. Indeed, capitalist systems have worked best where the laws are efficient, effective, and reinforced throughout society.

Capitalism's notion of private property is being undermined and destroyed by the digital economy. What is arising are small, large, and massive collaborations among people who know and don't know each other, participating without being paid to create something of value. Collaborations such as Wikipedia, Linux, Wordpress, Drupal, and Sugar CRM are examples of massive collaborations. Social movements around the world are lived and shared through online communities. Artists are creating collectives with people in different cities to collaborate to bring their work to audiences.

[ii] Capitalists marketing ebooks admitted as much when they colluded to create a floor in the price of an ebook.

In fact, artists, activists, and internet marketers continue to "push the free line." Pushing the free line means opening more and more internet content to free distribution. Their goal is to make as much information, knowledge, and product as possible free to internet users, simultaneously diminishing the value of asserting property rights and undermining the market mechanism.

These early collaborationists assert rights to protect free collaborative products from capitalist appropriation. These "creative commons" rights are often used to protect the collaborative effort and preserve its ability to be used and accessed by anyone. But it is not hard to see that these nascent efforts are precursors to a new logic. Private property will become a quaint, old idea, and people will collaborate based on skill and desire, contributing to a greater good as a part of the emerging new world.

Capitalism cannot operate without a system of private property rights. The whole logic of investment, production, sales and marketing, return on investment, and pooling of capital relies on the notion of private property. "I invest in this, so I can produce it, sell it, make a profit, and go buy something else." None of those phrases make any sense if you cannot own what you invest in, create, sell, or buy. The accumulation of capital requires the ability to own that capital.

This change toward communal property ownership in the digital commons occurs as a result of digitalization, which is a natural creation of capitalism. It is not a progressive political reaction against abuse or oppression. I doubt the people collaborating on Wikipedia do so primarily as a social action against corporate capitalism. Rather, it seems to be a spontaneous activity—people working for free to add to a common good (in this case knowledge)—simply because that's what they want to do. This kind of activity is widespread among young people creating online communities primarily because they are interested. They create communities with structures, key roles, and the ability to contribute, all for free, while no one really owns it.

The Erosion of Capitalism

Trends can be profound liars, and in this analysis, I certainly do not want to imply that capitalism is currently on its last throes. It is not. And yet, capitalism's ongoing development appears to be eroding its own foundation. Where anti-capitalist movements have failed to actually change the system, capitalism's own intrinsic logic seems to be succeeding. Capitalism is poised to erode itself into non-being over time.

As this process unfolds, capitalism will go to great lengths to preserve the status quo. It will assert property rights more vigorously to protect ownership. It will develop pricing mechanisms to create a sense of scarcity and ensure profits. It will attempt to create new markets through free trade, more commercial intrusiveness, and relentless innovation. And, it will try to solve the global externality challenge through market mechanisms. However, what it cannot do is stop its own internal logic—relentless digitalization will continue and social collaboration will expand. As they do, capitalism will gradually lose its hegemonic hold on the collective economic imagination, and eventually give way to a very different world.

Four Dimensions Driving the Fall of Capitalism

Historical epochs don't change very often. Capitalism, which replaced feudalism in the 15th and 16th centuries, has dominated western culture ever since that time. As it grew and developed, capitalism changed legal structures, religion, the political sphere, and social relations. It changed the human relationships with nature and the environment, and also the way we think and perceive the world. The last five hundred years were required for this historical epoch to come to fruition.

When historical epochs end, the disruption tends to occur along similar lines. Today, capitalism is hitting its own crisis point as significant discontinuities mirror those that occurred when the feudal system was challenged by circumstances and capitalism came into being. In this essay, we will review four categories that drove the feudalism-to-capitalism transition, and identify current changes in the same categories which signal capitalism's susceptibility to major systemic change.

Four Dimensions in the Break with Feudalism

One account of the breakdown of feudalism as an economic system comes from Paul Mason in his book *Postcapitalism: A Guide to Our Future*. Mason outlines four main drivers in the decline of feudalism, summarized as follows:

- The Black Death hit Europe in the 1300s, and in the span of six years, it had killed a quarter of Europe's population. With 25 percent less people to work the fields, labor acquired new power over production, and the result was a destabilized social order spanning several decades.[5]
- Banking emerged and grew through the pre-Renaissance and Renaissance periods. Its acceptance and growth laid the financial roots for capitalism, while simultaneously undercutting the political power structures of feudal society.[6]
- The conquest of the Americas, including the pillage and plunder of gold and other treasures from the societies that were already there, resulted in the conquistadores' theft of 1.3 million ounces of gold.

The resulting new wealth fueled the rise of capitalism and the fall of feudalism as a virtual revolution swept through the European economies.[7]

- The invention of the printing press brought the written word to the masses for the first time, but with very profound consequences. The printing press not only enabled general literacy, it also undercut guild-based social structures by re-arranging labor relations in the new print shops.[8]

The process of historical change is long and gradual, and in Mason's descriptions, it is clear that the break with feudalism is no exception. The Black Death occurred between 1347 and 1353, the first printing press went into production in 1450, and the plunder of the Americas was a 16th century phenomena—in other words, it took at least 100 to 200 years for the transition to unfold. During that time, all spheres of life were transformed—economic, political, and social. Economically, it was a move from feudalism to capitalism, but it was also a much bigger move from medieval times to modernity.

As we move into the postcapitalist era, we can expect it will take time; but it will probably move much more quickly than the feudalism-to-capitalism transition. The current transition will also be multifaceted and reach far across the many realms of human existence—even into realms of which most of our culture is currently unaware. Economics, religion, and politics, yes; but we are due for a similar revolution of consciousness, attitude, social structures, and relationship with the natural environment. Profound disruptions like the end of capitalism's dominance create deep and wide-ranging change—so much so that we become, actually, different kinds of people.

The four factors Mason lays out can be categorized as changing technology, social structure challenges and change, new ideas, and exogenous shock. These categories are comprehensive in that they cut across all the spheres of human activity. They also give us a perspective on how far the change has developed, and what we might expect in the future.

Changing Technology

The printing press was the most profound technological change driving the transition to capitalism. It broke apart the religion-politics stranglehold on knowledge by spreading literacy to the masses. That literacy made the

Reformation possible because without it, Martin Luther could not have asserted a direct relationship with God by way of the Bible. Literacy moved the focal point of power from outside ecclesiastical authority to within the individual self, a move that enabled Calvin to leave the decisions on usury and merchant profiteering to the individual conscience rather than church or state law, thereby paving the way for individualized capitalism to develop.

If the most profound technological change accompanying the decline of feudalism was the printing press, the technological change driving the end of capitalism is digitalization. In addition to its direct economic impact, digitalization has changed our social practices and structures, how we measure and determine class, how markets operate, how social networks are built, our perceptions of our bodies, and even our relationships with company, country, and God.

Digitalized information is becoming the currency of the new postcapitalist economy. It isn't just that information is important; it is driving value up while making it impossible to price that value. While the economy will run on digitalized information, thereby making that information extremely valuable, digital products cannot be priced to reflect that value in classic capitalist terms. Such products can be copied endlessly with no cost, so supply is essentially infinite and free, and the products cannot carry price-based value—that is, so long as no single entity achieves a monopoly on distribution. Yet even here, the exception proves the rule. If monopolies are acceptable practice, capitalism is no longer functioning.

In a digitalized world, two things are likely to matter most: the ability to *process digits* and the ability to *connect digits*. Processing digits has come a very long way indeed. Few people realize that the $600 iPhone they carry around with them has approximately 120 million times more computing power than the multi-million dollar Apollo Guidance Computer that was used to put the first men on the moon.[9] That is a rapid change in computing power. What is today's equivalent? The supercomputer running *predictive* models of weather, markets, and human behavior, which is a far step above the computing power to calculate answers from data. Supercomputers will also shrink, and this will put the processing power of a supercomputer into the hands of millions within the next 50 to 100 years. Finally, processing power is changing in the form of artificial intelligence, which is quickly eclipsing the power of the best thinkers in the world, much as precision machinery eclipsed the best craftsmen in the world. In all these cases, quantum leaps are occurring in both the speed and the quantity of digits processed, and in those quantum leaps, new capabilities emerge which are extremely valuable.

The ability to *connect* digits is evident in two key aspects of the internet. The first aspect is the actual high-speed broadband internet lines, the networks of wireless communications, and the giant server farms hosting all that data, processing it, and providing its usefulness in storage and connectivity.

The second aspect is what is built on that infrastructure. These are the online networks like Facebook and Twitter, the software as a service (SaaS) models for business, like Salesforce.com or Marketo, and the communities of joint production, like Linux, Wordpress, Wikipedia, and even fan fiction. Some of these products are offered in a capitalist form as subscriptions, while others are totally free and one gets access over the internet.

As connection and processing speeds increase, as products are increasingly digitalized, and as new capabilities enable us all to change things in ways we cannot even foresee, qualitative changes will cascade through society because—just as they did with the printing press—these technological changes will alter social, political, economic, and religious relationships. Luther could not have led the Protestant Reformation without the printing press because it required people have their own copy of the Bible so they could read it. Descartes could not have popularized his vision of the mechanistic universe without the printing press either. Only history will tell us who the contemporary Luther and Descartes will turn out to be, but we can rely on that fact that whoever it is, their ideas, frameworks, and reshaping of human perception will not be possible without the digitalization of the economy and all the technology developing to support it.

Social Struggle and Change

The social struggle that accompanied the waning of feudalism was evident in the history of the period, including the religious massacres and Inquisitions, economic uprisings, land revolts, and outright political revolutions. Major shifts in civilization must include these struggles, and we should expect nothing less as postcapitalism emerges.

The social struggle befalling the end of capitalism will be different than anything anyone has ever imagined. It's not about the working class revolting as in the labor movements of the 19th and early 20th centuries, although there are elements of that. It's not a Marxist proletariat revolution against the bourgeoisie, although there are elements of that as well. Globalized capitalism, on the eve of the digitalization of everything, is facing a new and different challenge.

The Occupy movement, even though it didn't last long, illustrated some of the new dynamics. It showed that discontent with the global order is, in fact, global. Demonstrations broke out not only on Wall Street, but in cities across America, in Madrid, London, and Berlin, and in other cities throughout the world. Public discontent is ubiquitous because economic conditions are difficult, people cannot seem to make progress, and they feel increasingly enslaved by growing debt and stagnant wages.

This discontent is not reflected only in progressive global movements however. It is also expressed in the xenophobic rise of right wing ideas. Today, the Donald Trump phenomena both roils America and is expressing the real fears of ordinary people. Fascist ideas are rising again as people instinctively look for a figure who can "get us out of this mess." Germany, France, and Italy all have growing right wing parties, and Britain expressed its discontent by voting to withdraw from the European Union. These are all signs of the same social struggles.

The problem, however, goes beyond the West. China has hundreds of protests every day which we do not hear about in the West. ISIS is possible only because of the profound discontent among the people it recruits—from the streets of Muslim dominated cities like Peshawar to the immigrant neighborhoods of Paris, Brussels, and Minneapolis. Japan has stagnated for decades, and Russia has embraced its own strongman in Putin.

In all these cases, what is different and what ties it all together is the global network. Never before in history was that possible. Digitalization is creating novel social structures that enable people in these far flung locations to connect, communicate, and most importantly, belong. In each case, there is a profound sense of powerlessness in these global locations—and the universal complaint is an attempt to gain control or power over their own circumstances. Capitalism created globalization. It profoundly disempowered nearly all people, but so far, that disempowerment has been felt and expressed largely at the margins, while the social center stands bewildered by it all. But the force of globalization is shrinking the center, just as it was designed to do. Bewilderment is giving way to commitment, and people are lining up on different ends of the spectrum to challenge the dominant capitalist order.

Social struggles will find various manifestations as people try to find a way to thrive, but in their frustration, social struggle may easily become social strife. If it does, it will almost certainly center on the condemnation of the other, defined through race, ethnicity, religion, sexual orientation, or some other differentiating feature. Yet the strife will also be driven by new class distinctions having to do with access to networks, novel invention, and real economy access—i.e., food, water, clothing, shelter. The difference between those who have wealth and access versus those who do not is likely to remain a major dividing line, and the pressures for migration will force these groups together.

A good example of the social change lies in the work and religion relationship. If digitalization devalues or eliminates work, the religious doctrines that rose to reinforce capitalism will disintegrate—and they may be disintegrating already. Religious notions against idleness, for example, celebrate the sanctity of productive work. Success is understood in religious terms as a blessing from God, thereby implying that the non-successful are not as loved by the same God. These doctrines can be upheld so long as work leads to money and to participation in the economy. But a breakdown in that possibility opens the door to very different religious doctrines.

When the devaluation of work becomes a mass experience, the indoctrinated will be at a loss. What am I to do? What is life for? Have we been tricked? How do we eat? These existential questions will arise, and religion will need to find answers. For some, the answers appear in a regression to pre-modern thought patterns, worldviews, and doctrines. They will find solace in various forms of fundamentalism, believing somehow that very old books have the answers to what ails them. For others, there will be a re-assessment of the religious texts and doctrines, looking for new and different meanings. And for a third group, we may see an increase in consciousness—a new spirituality that does not rely on moral rules, codes of ethics, clergy intermediaries, or other traditions, but rather on awakening consciousness. Digitalization will open new vistas of perception and we may expect a consciousness revolution to bring true consciousness out of the rhetoric of the alternative and into the mainstream. It remains to be seen which route wins the hearts and minds of people at mass scales, but all three will be active through the confusion and difficulty of the coming period.

New Ideas

The third element driving feudal collapse and the rise of capitalism was new ideas and principles. Chief among these were notions of the private ownership of property, the relocation of sovereignty from a king or nobleman to the masses and to individuals, and the rule of law. Protestantism disintermediated one's relationship with God, making clergy largely unnecessary. Perhaps the most innovative legal idea was the invention of the corporation. Many of these ideas, which seem so basic to us today, were the source of enormous, long drawn-out political, religious, and military battles over hundreds of years. Some were social battles--massacres, witch hunts, and burnings at the stake occurred in the name and defense of these ideas.

And yet, it did not stop there. Science introduced all new ideas and processes, and the imagination of the machine developed. Capital and labor came to be understood as guiding concepts, and all these ideas promulgated themselves into society at all levels. So thorough has been the indoctrination that today in America, it seems that everything comes down to money—as if there is no other value worth valuing. But at the time when capitalism was replacing feudalism, these were all revolutionary ideas.

So, where are our revolutionary ideas today?

We are at a very nascent stage of new ideas. Political and economic rhetoric are drawing mostly on old ideas—the strongman to save us, xenophobia, socialist principles, and the power of central planning. Most of the truly new ideas are yet to come, but we can see possibilities.

As one example, the internet has spawned the much wider use of a legal idea called the Creative Commons. This idea allows people to publish and freely redistribute content that they did not create themselves, provided they simply give appropriate credit to the author and do not sell it. No royalties, no payments. Content leaders using the internet have advanced content to create and establish networks.

This notion of a creative commons, however, is revolutionary in terms of capitalism because it begins to undercut the core principle of private property. It suggests that there is a commons into which creative work may be contributed, and that, while there is value there, no one can sell it. While individual artists, authors, thinkers, and musicians may use the Creative

Commons in their own ways, the same idea supports the collaborative work of Wikipedia and similar online communities.

A second nascent idea is a new form of corporate organization. For hundreds of years, the normal C Corporation evolved from a special privilege granted only for public purpose to a ubiquitous organizational form. It has gained its power primarily from excluding everything from consideration other than profit, the accumulation of capital, and the deployment of capital, all in the shareholder interest. It motivated boards, executives, employees, and suppliers to focus only on those outcomes. Not only was this a cultural issue, it was a legal issue. Everyone involved had fiduciary responsibilities to serve shareholder interests.[iii]

Critics of the corporation, including myself, have long noted that so long as the structure of the corporation involves these inherent biases, it will not be able to create change. One response was to create the new B Corporation—a for-profit corporation with all the benefits of traditional incorporation, but which could also include public benefit into its charter and bylaws, thereby accomplishing two things: the expansion of responsibilities for leaders, and relief from the burden of focusing all energy *only* on profit and capital accumulation—a change in the inherent behavior broadly practiced today.

Almost thirty states have adopted statutes to allow the formation of B Corporations, and the list is growing. Far more than national health insurance or the social safety net, this idea alone could produce a dramatic, albeit long-term, change in society. Leaders have not been allowed to allocate corporate resources to public benefit in the past; now, boards and executives can determine the goods they want to create outside the C Corporation restrictions, and can apply the resources accordingly, without fear of a lawsuit for breach of fiduciary responsibility to shareholders.

[iii] Note that several commentators, including Robert Reich, have asserted in recent books that this was not always understood as a shareholder responsibility issue. They cite the 1940s to 1970s as a time when CEOs saw a bigger picture and comported themselves to serve that bigger picture. Even if we grant that may be true, both the preceding and subsequent periods in which shareholder interests were the only thing that matters illustrates the structural bias. There can always be inspired leaders or cultural norms against exclusive focus on shareholder returns, but there will never be resistance to that focus from the legal framework of the corporation. In fact, corporate structure will push CEOs and the rest of the corporate staff in that direction.

Let's be clear: this new power could be used for good or for ill. What one person sees as a "public benefit," another may see as public harm. Many debates will play out among these ideas, but there is no doubt that, as B Corporations catch on and become a major form of business organization, the relentless drive to profit and capital accumulation will be relativized. Mission statements will be more than mere HR tools for rallying the troops and "capturing their hearts," and the impact of business structures in the waning days of capitalism may be very different indeed.

A third relatively nascent idea is the so-called Gospel of Abundance. This notion has become near doctrine in certain conservative evangelical churches, new age spiritual circles, and even the personal development realm. Although far from a defining doctrine for the culture today, it may hold the seeds of the doctrine religion will use to replace the vaunted Protestant work ethic. At its core, this notion states, *the world is an abundant and giving place, and it has blessed me by giving me what I have.* The idea is to expect abundance to bless you, but also to provide permission to enjoy it. The blessings are decidedly divorced from any sense of earning it. Maybe you worked and maybe you didn't, but clearly you were blessed, so be grateful. Although I am quite certain those who promulgated this notion never intended it, there could hardly be a better doctrinal idea for the eventual acceptance of postcapitalist ideas like universal basic income.

Just as new ideas proliferated during the Renaissance and as feudalism gave way to capitalism, new ideas are appearing throughout the world and at all levels of society today. When digitalization provides new metaphors such as networks, open source, and the conversion of energy, new areas of human imagination open up. From there, the new ideas emerge that will guide and determine the future of human civilization.

Exogenous Shocks

Feudalism had the Black Death; capitalism has climate change. So far, climate change has not become an exogenous shock because the effects are largely localized and gradual, but that is likely to change.

Around 1350, the Black Death wiped out 25 percent of Europe's people.[10] This tipped the balance of the feudal system irretrievably. The shortage of labor gave the workers an economic advantage, and that destabilized the system. Labor did not win in the end, but this change in the power structure initiated changes in the system. Long running mutual allegiances between land owner and serf—allegiances that were the bond of the system—fell away, and new structures had to appear. These new structures initiated capitalism.

Today, many sources of exogenous shock are possible. The possibilities include everything from nuclear annihilation to ecosystem collapse, GMO releases gone bad, and financial collapse that cannot be socialized. While these are all possible, the most likely source remains climate change. Climate change is going to disrupt capitalism because it is an inevitable result of capitalism. As climate change occurs, centers of productive agriculture will change, areas now full of people will become uninhabitable, and activities previously unthinkable in some areas will become newly possible. Massive migration will almost certainly result, and it will deeply challenge governments and people.

We can also expect a technology shock that will challenge society in novel ways—the development and deployment of robots and artificial intelligence. Digitalization, of course, is the foundation for these developments, but robots and artificial intelligence are going to change who we are as people. Already, a small number of kids are growing up interacting with robots, and as they are socialized to the robot, expectations regarding human interactions are changing. Kids with these experiences frequently report that they *prefer* interacting with the robot because it is safe—thereby simplifying their perception of what to expect in interactions, and not equipping them for the difficulties of dealing with real people.[11]

As robots take over labor, and artificial intelligence takes over thinking, we will face a new kind of existential crisis—what are people supposed to do? This will be existential because capitalism provides an answer: work, earn money, and buy things. But if robots do the work, you can't earn money or buy things. Then what? To the capitalist mind, which nearly all of us share, this will come as a terrible shock.

Both of these shocks—climate change and the displacement of labor with robots and AI—are inevitable because they are the *result* of capitalism. Both are classified as exogenous because they result from the unaccounted externalities on which capitalism depends. Climate change results from accumulated pollution, and displacement of labor is a social externality that is irrelevant to capitalism's function. Ironically, these externalities will destroy capitalism. Capitalism cannot survive if we cook the human race off the planet, nor can it survive if we keep the people but they cannot buy its stuff. Either one of these shocks will be enough to create dramatic change and play a key role in the postcapitalist world that will emerge.

Forward with Our Eyes Open

The current global culture is facing all four dimensions of change at the same time. The feudalism-to-capitalism transition was fueled by these same four dimensions, and the change was characterized by social, religious, and political strife. Religious massacres, mass revolutions, and civil revolts were as much a part of it as was the flowering freedoms and the early stages of liberty, science, egalitarianism, and economic dynamism.

There is no reason to believe that our contemporary transition will be devoid of similar phenomena. In fact, we probably already see it. Massacres are becoming an awful but expected part of modern life. Anxiety over our well-being is giving rise to reactionary political movements. Religion seems to be a non-force, except when it hails to some backward-looking safety of ancient texts, and then projects hatred against all those who see it differently. Likewise, tremendous benefits in human creativity, morality, political organization, and other spheres will also result. In other words, we can anticipate a similar dynamic today as what happened five hundred years, but with more rapidity, comprehensiveness, and global reach.

Speculating on the future is critical to anticipating its eventuality. By imagining the transition and this new future, we can anticipate it and respond to it before and as it happens. The reactions characterizing the feudalism-to-capitalism transition occurred most acutely as people became victims of the change. Through anticipation, we can move from victim to guide, and with any luck, prevent some of the most disturbing side effects of the transition that lies ahead.

One Hundred Years to Real Postcapitalism

Three Stages of Transition

Historical transitions typically take a very long time to unfold, and the transition from postcapitalism to capitalism is just such a transition. The reason they take so long—and will even in the digital age of lightning fast communication and diffusion of ideas—is that the entrenched powers of the old system require a long time to unwind. This is especially true of capitalism. Large capitalist enterprises and infrastructure, for example, represent enormous investments made over many decades, and even centuries. These cannot be unwound quickly, and the people responsible for them will resist the unwinding as well. Although they will eventually give way to the new digitalized world, these realities always slow the process.

In this essay, we explore three likely stages of transition. These stages are necessarily general, speculative, and lacking in clear delineation. Nonetheless, they are conceptually helpful as a lens to clarify what history shows us. The stages are likely to unfold over the course of 100 years, give or take a few decades, and reflect trends that will arise and tend to dominate in each period. Let's see what each stage involves.

Early Transition—Capitalist Desperation

First, in the early stages, the elite capitalists will cling to power. Perceiving a threat to their wealth, they will look for every possible way to control the outputs of the digital economy. They will use and develop intellectual property law, continue to assert market-based models as solutions to intransigent problems, and continue to accumulate and concentrate wealth at the very top, especially in those areas where they are successful controlling the digital capital, as they see it. This trend is likely to continue for two to three decades as the capitalist powers consolidate returns and seek to hold on to what they have.

Financialization of the economy will continue in this early period. Financialization (which has also been called rentism) refers to the conversion from producing and selling products and services for cash to creating income through rent, interest, dividend investments, and subscribed automated services. This conversion will continue for most middle- and upper-middle-class people as the value of their work deteriorates and they seek income through non-work financial arrangements. More and more people will find a way to financialize their lives, thereby creating unearned income streams which are one precursor to the non-work, non-priced digital economy.

While the people at the top will cling to their gains, and people in the upper-middle classes will financialize to experience abundance, the brunt of the negative changes will be felt from the middle to lower classes at varying degrees. Most of these people will lose income-producing work to the early robots and other digital changes to the economy because this work is the easiest to automate. At the same time, they will have to rent nearly everything needed in life—housing, transportation, their own genes, and even ideas.

Today, global competition suppresses wage growth, but as digitalization reduces the pricing power of goods, the market price for labor approaches zero, as well. Capitalists will try to ensure the prices for goods at market do not go to zero, but no one will stop the accompanying reduction in wages.[iv] Capitalists will engage a certain kind of arbitrage between the declining price of labor and the not-yet-declining price of goods and services that low- and middle-income earners need. Those whose labor is their chief value and income will be squeezed, and the already large gap between the wealthy and everyone else will become even wider.

Middle Stage—Meaningless Money and UBI

The middle stage of the transition will be characterized by efforts to preserve the meaning of money and prevent its eventual collapse. Digitalization is often understood as an artifact of technology, but what it really represents is the migration of value into the digital components of products and services. Ebooks and recorded music have their value almost 100% in the digits, and because the marginal cost of reproduction is zero, prices in a market collapse to zero as well.

[iv] This actually happened when Amazon, Apple, and other ebook publishers collaborated to create a pricing floor for ebooks at the very vanguard of the postcapitalist trend. See Jeff Roberts' "The E-book Investigations: Are Publishers and Apple Breaking the Law?" (https://gigaom.com/2011/12/07/419-the-e-book-investigations-are-publishers-and-apple-breaking-the-law/).

Today, products like coffee mugs and cars still have substantial value located in their physical being, but as 3D printing, robotics, and similar technologies improve, the value will shift from the thing itself to the plan for the thing. But the plan will be in digits, and that digital component will collapse in price just like digital music does and for the same reason—infinite supply and zero cost of reproduction. In other words, all products are becoming predominantly digital, and those that aren't are being produced with automated robotic labor.

Let's think about what this means. In a world where digitalization and robot labor eliminate the cost of human labor, they also eliminate demand. If people don't have wages, they cannot buy goods and services. As economies have become increasingly driven by consumption, this change will be extremely disruptive, and the capitalists will feel the heat. As the consumption class is decreasingly capable of consuming at the standard economic level, it will become impossible for capitalists to get a return on investment. Hence, the whole paradigm for deploying capital, as well as the financialization of life, will become meaningless, and financial wealth will collapse.

As a defense against this collapse, capitalist elites will advocate the actual emergence of universal basic income (UBI) for everyone. Under UBI, all citizens receive an income from the government, whether they work or not. You could think of it as social security for everyone. If this comes about, it won't be because of a rising leftist political power or a sudden urge to end poverty. Instead, it will be capitalists who lead this movement as a way to preserve demand and protect profits. Elon Musk and Mark Zuckerberg are talking seriously about this, and even the prominent bond investor Bill Gross has called for it in his investment outlooks. This outcome is the logical result of digitalization, and it is the only way for capitalists to hold off the total collapse of their wealth and maintain the relevance of money.

Nonetheless, the collapse of wealth will come, and it will be a defining moment. While the havoc on our economic institutions can hardly be overestimated, we are actually facing a collapse that is both *qualitative* and *quantitative*. The 2008 collapse was quantitative—a fact easily understood by considering its signature solution, so-called "quantitative easing." Central bankers created trillions of dollars, and in so doing, saved capitalism. UBI is essentially quantitative easing for the common citizen. Like the bank-targeted quantitative easing of 2008 to 2015, UBI will be created with invented money. It will be an attempt to hold off the inevitable, and just as the bank-based quantitative easing held it off for a while, UBI will, too. In this second phase of the postcapitalist era, we can expect to see a continued, quantitative widening of the income and wealth gap in the short-term, but in the longer term we are likely to see a decrease in the meaning of that gap as the economy becomes more focused on free goods and services.

Here's the qualitative problem: What good is it to have all the money in the world if everything is free and nothing can be purchased anyway? It isn't that the capitalists will lose their money; their problem will be that the capital they accumulated will become increasingly worthless. It will provide them with decreasing levels of power and influence. Buying and investing become meaningless because goods and services cannot be sold at a price. In other words, the capitalist measures of value will no longer work. In a world of free digital products and services, there is no point to earning money—not by labor nor by deployment of capital. You wouldn't be able to use the money anyway. This will be a crisis point because, almost inevitably, the new postcapitalist value system will have yet to emerge.

Final Stage—New Measures of Value

Full transition will be marked by a change in the metrics of value. It's impossible to predict the new measures for certain, but it is likely that the familiar measures of dollars, wages, and profit, for example, will no longer dominate. In an economic system where markets cannot function, what does profit mean? Who would pay wages for labor to build something that can't be sold? If everything is automated, what does labor mean? No doubt, these terms could receive a revised meaning in popular usage, but if so, they certainly won't retain the same economic meaning.

More to the point, a whole new system of economic measures, religious values, and socio-political structures is likely to emerge. Many people are speculating and hoping that the postcapitalist economy will be one of full automation, UBI, and digital abundance of nearly everything. In essence, the dream is that all basic needs are taken care of by an automatic economy, and people will be freed to live their creativity. Optimists celebrate this dream, while capitalist critics decry the lost incentive to work. To me, both look rather idealistic, and the reality is likely to be something far different than nearly anyone can imagine.

For example, the capitalist criticism of basic income is that it removes the incentive for wage labor, as if work is inherently a good thing. In a capitalist value system, work most certainly is a good thing, and that judgement was reinforced by religious values honoring the essential place of work in capitalist life. But in a postcapitalist world, work loses its value. Perhaps creativity emerges, perhaps love emerges, perhaps social balkanization emerges—but the central value of wage labor will deteriorate and disappear. (If it hasn't, then we have not yet passed into the final stage of the transition to postcapitalism.) Today, work is so important that it determines our socioeconomic status, our opportunity, the communities we live in and schools our kids go to, and how the intrinsic biases of the law treat us. If no one has to work, this entire capitalist social structure must change, and what it changes to will become evident at this stage.

So what new values might emerge? Here are a few ideas:

- Influence as measured by the ubiquity and diffusion of ideas—the more they spread, the more valuable they are.
- Connectedness as measured by involvement in networks.
- Adoption and usage of free products built by collaborative communities or solopreneurs
- Ease of life
- Quality of experiences

These are just a few brainstorms—the list could be endless, but it will always tie back to the new metaphors of a postcapitalist world. Notice how different these terms are from profit, money, capital, and return on investment, which dominate the capitalist view of value.

The world after capitalism will no longer recognize the most basic principles of capitalism—the value of work, capital, private property, rule of law, and perhaps even the sovereignty of the individual. Indeed, new visions of freedom may move past the Enlightenment view that, as Immanuel Kant said, "man is free if he needs to obey no person but solely the laws."[12] When these notions erode, the only option remaining will be to imagine a new world. Some will fight to retain some of the old values, while others work to create the new ones. This battle will feel to many like the world is coming apart. That's because the principles at stake stand as the very bedrock of modern capitalist society—so much so that we cannot imagine the world any other way. People will worry about and decry these eventualities in many books, essays, speeches and sermons. But in the end, the transition to postcapitalism will be recognized by the dissolution of capitalism's core principles, and the emergence of new measures of value.

Zen Acceptance

As the world changes radically through digitalization, we can respond with fear or with radical acceptance. I recommend the latter. Radical acceptance enables us to see the world for what it is, shape the changes ahead, and not fear it. Already as the changes unfold, we can see some of the most likely structures emerging—collaboration, networks, the free economy, digital abundance, and the automation of work. We will not go back to the servitude of feudalism, nor to the subservience of capitalism. Indeed, perhaps the most radical reform of all in the postcapitalist society will be the inability to support the top-down hierarchy of capitalistic structure. In feudalism, we had lords and serfs; in capitalism, we have bosses and workers. Although qualitatively different, the social structure of hierarchical power is little changed. Religion still celebrates obedience because capitalism requires an obedient population. Postcapitalism will not be complete until hierarchy is marginalized and obedience as a value is destroyed. The mystery, suspense, and joy lie in watching for what emerges in its place.

Why Thought Matters: Paving the Road to Transition

The history of capitalism in the western world demonstrates the critical role of ideas in directing the general flow of capitalism, as well as the assumed role ideas will play in developing a new postcapitalist era. In 1776, close to the dawn of the Industrial Revolution, Adam Smith published *An Inquiry into the Nature and Causes of the Wealth of Nations,* which became the definitive text of capitalist thought at the time. In many ways, Smith's work was the culmination of a hundred years of thought going back at least to John Locke's treatises, which worked out the philosophy of private property, and extending through decades of pitched debates in Enlightenment thinking. No doubt the French philosophes had many other concerns in their Enlightenment-era debates than an emerging economic structure, but those same debates and ideas played a major role in changing the ideology behind the continued development of capitalist thought. Indeed, the Enlightenment, which transfixed European thought for most of the 18th century, provided an objective way of thinking that made the new industrial capitalism possible. The more the matters of the world were separated from matters of religion, the more the ground was established for a totally secular capitalism to take hold. In other words, capitalism needed an appropriate thought environment for it to thrive.

The capitalist thought environment of the eighteenth century, however, was both deeper and broader than Smith's work. The Christian Reformation, for example, was very significant in unleashing capitalism two centuries earlier. The first religious doctrines associated with the Reformation actually opposed capitalism in no uncertain terms (see Martin Luther's writing or R.H. Tawney's explanation in *Religion and the Rise of Capitalism*).[13] The moral compass Luther provided had more to do with the individual's relationship to God, thereby severing the intricate medieval relationship between individual, church, and society which had kept rampant capitalism at bay. Luther's intent was not to unleash capitalism, but it became a significant part of his legacy.

After Luther, John Calvin developed Luther's doctrines into ideas that ushered in capitalism. In Calvin's work, it became justifiable to collect interest on debt—an activity frowned upon as usury by church and moral society up to that point. Although Calvin provided many limitations that the believer should consider, it remained up to the individual human being to provide his own moral compass. This change suddenly undid all the prohibitions against usury, as well as other social and moral customs constraining markets, and it freed debt to be not only operative, but far more ubiquitous, in society.

Luther and Calvin are examples of how the thought environment changes the social structure and approach to how we understand the world. At one point, usury is a sin and an activity largely unacceptable, yet one hundred years later, it is viewed as essential to the economy, and those who use debt are celebrated in the religious and social fabric of society. A similar transformation occurred with merchant trade, which went from having deep moral restrictions against selling traded items at too high a price or profiting from scarcity, to a world in which traders are expected to sell according to market dynamics.

More recently than the Renaissance and Enlightenment examples just given, neoliberalism developed its own "common sense" framework over many decades before the neoliberal project really unfolded in the 1980s. Leo Strauss and the Austrian School of Economics are often cited as the initiators of the ideological framework of neoliberalism in the 1930s,[14,15] but as in the Enlightenment, the ideas developed over decades, were often hotly debated, and did not come to the fore until Ronald Reagan and Margaret Thatcher came to power in the 1980s. Just as the philosophes of the Enlightenment built their encyclopedia, publication companies, and institutions of study, the neoliberals started think tanks, took positions of political power, and established positions in existing and new institutions. They promulgated their ideas, and eventually made them "obvious." It was Reagan who famously said "government is not the solution to our problem; government is the problem,"[16] but in actuality, he was mouthing words that the neoliberals had been arguing over for decades.

A Postcapitalist Thought Environment

Capitalism needed these changes in the thought environment before it could blossom; the postcapitalist era needs similar changes. A thought environment, as I mean it, is an environment of ideas which define the direction of the economic or social system. A thought environment determines what most people would address as "common sense" or "reality." Ideas expressed in this area tend to present themselves as underlying assumptions, and when everyone agrees, you can be sure that thought has not occurred, but the thought environment is defining reality. For example, how many well-meaning parents have implored their children to find work they enjoy "because you'll be doing it for the next 50 years!" How many of us know that whenever demand goes up, prices go up? It is a "known fact" of economic reasoning—nevermind that it is only true under certain situations in which supply is limited. Consider this: as the population increases on earth, the demand for air goes up; we all need to breathe. Why don't we see an increase in price then? Because air doesn't fit the assumptions of the scarcity-based economic model.

If the coming challenge to capitalism is going to result in changes for the betterment of humanity, we need to start that decades-long thinking process now. We need ideas and imagination for what that new world will become, or we will face utter chaos if no replacement thought environment is in place. Human beings need thought to center themselves, and if we confront the coming challenges without pre-thought, we are doomed to a merely reactive stance simply because there is no alternative.

Competitors for the Thought Environment

There are four primary schools of thought regarding a postcapitalist future. The first is the predictable resistance from entrenched capitalist interests to the very idea of a postcapitalist era. It is based on denial and aggravated attempts to control. This group will fight to protect capitalist wealth and the system that created it, much like the lords fought to protect their feudal wealth 500 years ago. These are the voices arguing everything is impossible, everything must be privately owned, and climate change—a direct result of capitalism—is a fraud. Ultimately, these forces will fail, but they will delay the process.

The second school of thought endangering postcapitalism derives from the long historical resistance to capitalism itself. Consider these the anticapitalists, socialists, and communists. This school opposes capitalism altogether and sees hope in the digital disruption for a victory over capitalism. They hope that as the dynamics play out, the replacement system will align with long-held oppositional value. They hope to build a democratic socialism in the place of collapsing capitalism.

The problem with these idealistic hopes is that any form of socialism or communism we can imagine is just as dependent on the capitalist view of the world as capitalism is. Socialism has no more intrinsic values to align with the new digital metaphors than capitalism does. All three of these systems—communism, socialism, and capitalism—are built around industrial economic models that will soon be disrupted. The truth is that they will all meet the same fate, so turning to them for the alternative is a fool's game.

The third school of thought derives primarily from the business community. These are the people who are actually building the digital world as we know it. Think of Jeff Bezos, Steve Jobs, and Larry Ellison, as well as the millions of people trying to use the promise of digits to make their own living—from game creators to app builders to digital authors. These innovators approach the new world as one of incredible opportunity. They are building the networks, the collaborative communities, and the artificial intelligence that is driving the new world. Implicit in their work are assumptions about what is right and how the world works. Some think of these things carefully, morally, and with the social order in mind. Far more think of the possibilities of disruption and what that means in terms of capitalist profit. They are writing about ideas like "long tails", the promise of automation, and digital wonders, but only from their own perspective in most cases. There is little deep thinking about the impact on the social order, on our moral view of ourselves as individuals and society, nor about what happens to democracy in a non-capitalist world. Rather, the focus is on executing the disruption through the capitalist prism of business.

This group is not to be blamed for a lack of thought; they are doing what they do well—changing the world. They are working within the capitalist thought environment and structure, and as they do so, its own logic is driving this change, and they are therefore leaders of it. However, it stands to reason that if no alternative is developed, these habits of thought around execution are all that we will have. Because we can see all the other problems with modern society, following such a path does not appear particularly promising.

A fourth alternative view is arising from those who see the possibility of freedom in a postcapitalist world of abundance, no work, full automation, and universal basic income (UBI). Yet most of the readings I have seen in this area tend to focus on the *should*. We *should* have universal basic income. We *should* have full automation so no one has to work. We *should* be able to pursue our passions. While these *shoulds* may be laudable ideas, they don't help build the thought environment necessary to make them actually occur. It is kind of like walking up to an empty lot and shouting "I demand that a house be built here!" The shouter is probably correct, but the shouting doesn't build the house. That is a much more intricate, long-term project that requires real skill, planning, thought, understanding, and execution.

All of these schools of thought will compete to make substantial contributions to the thought environment for the postcapitalist era. Those contributions will be necessary, but they will not be sufficient. The real changes will happen through careful examination of the assumptions of our capitalist society, rethinking them, engaging what is possible, and discovering moral, psychological, and social structures which will underpin the new postcapitalist world. Some of these ideas have begun to be developed; the increasing realization among business and financial elites that UBI may be the only way to maintain an active economy; the articulation of alternatives to work; and the development of new modes of ownership. There is more, but they are largely underdeveloped and certainly not mainstream yet. Nonetheless, this is the work driving real change, and to which all effective change agents are called.

How Will We Define the New Postcapitalist Thought Environment?

Thought environments develop over time and there is no way to accurately predict specific outcomes. Nonetheless, some of the structural faults along which the new ideas will emerge can be ascertained, and some of the signals indicating that capitalism is being replaced by a new postcapitalist world can be surmised as well. Here are some likely faultlines and their accompanying signals.

First, in a postcapitalist world, the traditional left-right lens on society will be an anachronism in which both perspectives will barely achieve the status of quaint museum pieces. I'm not saying those views won't be present, nor that they won't contest with each other. It's just that both will be woefully inadequate to the task of establishing a new common sense. They can't because, by definition, they are creatures of capitalist thought. In other words, everything on the spectrum from Ayn Rand to Karl Marx is equally irrelevant to creating a thought environment for the postcapitalist era because the entire spectrum is part of capitalism's thought environment. Although it is too early to say exactly what will replace the left-right perspective, this signal occurs when left-right distinctions become confusing or meaningless and a new paradigm arises in the culture to explain and frame postcapitalist society.

Second, the constant referral to markets as an organizing principle will end. Some markets will continue to persist to enable people to trade goods and services. But they will not dominate everything in a postcapitalist view of the world. Today, in a market society, we assume that the economy operates on a law of supply and demand. The assumption is so strong that we actually call it a law. But in a world of abundant or infinite supply, that law—which depends on scarcity—breaks down. The question is: How does a world based on abundance actually operate? What "laws" emerge to help us understand how a new world of abundance will operate? The development of answers to these questions, and their diffusion throughout society, will also signal that we are moving into a postcapitalist society.

Third, in today's capitalism, it is assumed and accepted that everyone who *can* work for money *should* work for money. What would the world look like if we changed the assumption to say that *no one* should work for money—as if working for money is crass, crude, and primitive. Instead, there is an ethic that people should find ways to pursue their own passions and interests as a matter of their life purpose, not pejoratively as a "hobby." What might a world without work actually look like? What mechanisms would drive it? How might it actually emerge from the development of capitalistic experience and development? The signal of a rising postcapitalist thought environment will be clear when new attitudes toward work evolve, and experiences like the shame of unemployment or being stuck in a career you don't want vanish.

Fourth, we can imagine a society in which marking up the value of one person's work by another is reviled as an exploitation rather than celebrated as a profitable outcome. This core function of capitalism—to turn exploitation of labor into a socially acceptable practice—will disappear in a truly postcapitalist paradigm. In all likelihood, contribution will replace exploitation (profit) as the socially endorsed practice of leaders, and relaxation will replace rejuvenation as the prime value of the people capitalism calls workers. Exploitation requires rejuvenation, or people burn out. Contribution, on the other hand, engenders relaxation and balance. The signal to look for is a reduction in the ubiquity of the rejuvenation paradigm among workers—a reduction that has already begun.

Conclusion

Because of the radical disruption of the capitalist model and the merging digital metaphors, new ideas will emerge to usher in the postcapitalist era. New practices, capabilities, and realities will not only force new thinking, but may do so suddenly as old structures collapse. It will behoove us to proactively create the new thought environments so that we can shape the future and what our world will become.

The Imagination of the Digit

Historical epochs are typically associated with the economic, political, and religious systems that accompany them. Feudalism, for example, was characterized by monarchies, landed nobility, religious authority, and the appropriation of wealth through customary rents. Capitalism is characterized by democracy, Christianity, corporate concentration of power, and the exploitation of labor. Each epoch, however, can also be characterized by its own theme of imagination—i.e., the central metaphor around which most other ideas revolve. Feudalism envisioned an animated world of spirits and angels in which the world was very much alive, and this affected attitudes toward exploitation, use of resources, and reciprocal obligation. The capitalist period has been dominated by Descartes' image of the mechanistic universe in which the world is a dead machine that operates by laws and forces, not gods or spirits. Today, we can see that the postcapitalist period we are about to enter will hold the digit as its dominant metaphor. This essay makes a preliminary inquiry into what such an imagination of the digit might mean.

Digitalized Reimagination

The imagination of the digit is fundamentally different from capitalism's guiding image of the machine. The mechanistic view is linear, even if you include feedback loops. People draw business processes, for example, as shown below:

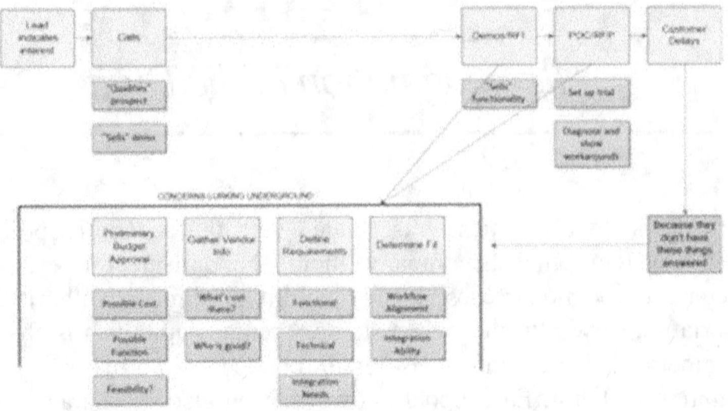

Figure 1. Sample business process diagram from Signorelli Consulting Group, Inc., 2016.

Step by step, a product is manufactured or a service provided. This linear template, however, goes far beyond business. It overlays natural systems, it defines the human being's self-image, and it explains how kids are "educated." Everything can be understood through this linear vision of the world.

In contrast, the imagination of the digit is decidedly non-linear. Digits may be strung together in an infinite numbers of ways and produce just as many different meanings. Then, they are launched into the digitalized world where they flow into vast networks. Where the mechanistic universe effectively controlled this flow, digital imagination opens it, as seen in the next image:

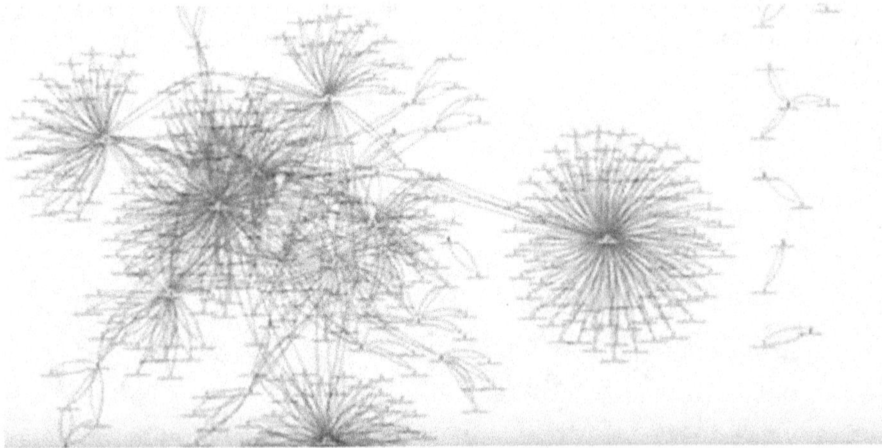

Figure 2. Example of a generic graph analytics data image common to big data analytics.

Digits and data are created by people or sensors. Data then flows into a node in the network, and it moves exponentially throughout that network. In social networks, it continues so long as people in the network remain interested. In data networks, it moves to wherever there is need for useful analysis. The loss of interest or analysis begins to limit flow, and at that point, the digits become dormant—at least until interest rises again.

Capitalism is best understood by analyzing process, whereas the postcapitalist world will be comprehended through networks. It is no wonder that a process driven system would result in an assembly line or a robotic factory. It is also no wonder that a digitized, networked world would create open source software and collaborative digital communities. But let's take it a step further. Capitalism's process is contained—one can own or control a process—and the improvement of an owned process is the key to higher competitiveness and success. Nearly all successful business people understand this.

As digitalization increases, digits are readily created, but they are notoriously difficult to control. Without control, it is impossible to compete. Instead, digits are giving rise to collaborative communities. No ownership, no competition. This is a fundamentally different way of thinking.

What would it be like if we used digits and networks as our guiding metaphor for life on earth? We know that life feeds on life. Under capitalism, this reality could only be understood as a competitive struggle to survive. Darwin's observation of the survival of the fittest was less an observation of nature than it was a view limited by the lens of competitive capitalist culture. What if nature were viewed through a networked lens? Would we see it differently if the framework was that collaborative communities occur all over the natural world, as opposed to ecosystems? Could it be that organisms provide for one another and contribute to a greater collaborative good? Does this lens matter?

I wonder as well how we might reimagine the human brain. Today, it is all about pathways, neurons, electrical charges, and neurotransmitters. Theoretically, blocks in the process cause mental and organic disease. But what if the brain is actually a network? Digits originate in the various sensors and nerve endings, then distribute exponentially and instantly through our brains. And what if it can go even further—beyond the material physiology into a more spiritual plane as many psychics have reported for centuries? It is easy to scoff at such a notion when viewed from the lens of controlled capitalist process. But if the world is an open network, does it become more possible to understand the so-called spiritual experience? After all, networks are infinite and so is spirit. Why shouldn't new doors of perception open with a new paradigm?

If we can reimagine nature and the brain, we might also reimagine enterprise. In some ways, we already have. Virtual business of many kinds are becoming the norm, as are business models driven by so-called gig employment, freelancers, and other independent agents. These examples, however, are still cut from the capitalist model. They may be less hierarchical in some ways, and more distributed for sure, but many still move by process and depend on cash and a certain amount of capital.

What else is possible? Could there be network-based business enterprises that are actually an alternative to the hierarchical, process-driven corporations? Could roles like worker, marketer, and CFO in a capitalist structure be replaced by more complete and holistic renaissance people connected in networks to create new possibilities? Will office buildings outlive their usefulness for housing people in proximity to one another when there is no need to be nearby? Can flowing digits replicate physical presence enough to make travel obsolete? These possibilities titillate the imagination—possibilities unimaginable in a process-driven world.

Waiting for the New Paradigm

Just as Descartes' mechanistic universe, capitalism's hierarchy, and principles like extraction, private property, and coercive labor guide our perceptions, the new networks, conversions, and collaborative communities will become ideas that shape how we see the world. The forefront of postcapitalist thought should be developing this new imagination of the digit.

Supercomputing: A Capitalist Response to the Postcapitalist Threat

Capitalism is on the defensive. Markets are failing. Automation is eliminating work. Digitalization is driving marginal production costs to zero. Private property is giving way to common, collaborative production and open-source ownership. But big capital isn't just giving in. It has every reason to protect its profits, maintain its advantages, and create more wealth. But if capitalist corporations are clinging to power, and digitalization is driving capitalism toward its own demise, how are the actors behaving to save their own capitalistic souls? It is simple—they are doubling down on capital and information. They are using supercomputers to process big data.

Business and Big Data

Big data consists of the massive amounts of data coming from the so-called internet of things, cell phone towers, human bodies, thousands of sensors in crash tests for automobiles, and millions of other sources. It is electronic, it is fast, and there is a lot of it. Many people bemoan the idea of big data as a creepy threat to privacy. Others see it as massively useful for tackling problems like the spread of flu virus every year. These perspectives may be true, but they do not explain the excitement in the business community for big data and its projects.

Why is business excited about big data? Because they can see both the relentless nature of digitalization, as well as its effects. Business leaders know that digital products have no marginal cost of production and infinite supply. They know that under those conditions, the price of that product declines rapidly toward zero in a supply and demand market. And they know that when prices are zero, the market economy can no longer function. For capitalist business leaders operating in such markets, they are facing industry Armageddon.

The business community believes that big data and supercomputing could be a savior. They realize that the value of digits isn't exactly zero; the digits retain a miniscule value. So, for capitalism and the business leader, big data is the quantitative, capitalistic response to digitalization—no more, and no less. It is the new feeder of the juggernaut; it aspires to be the power that will stop the slide to a free information economy. How does this work?

The capitalist premise of big data is this: if we can quickly gather enough data all at the same time and process it fast enough to enable a useful response, we can thwart the price slide toward zero. With enough digital data, we can hold a price, prevent the slide, and stave off the post-capitalist world. Of course, that's not exactly how it is said or thought about—people are not generally aware because business terminology cloaks it in words like added value, market response, or better meeting of customer demand. Employees talk and think that way, managers guide that way, and leaders express their visions in the same terms. But the real driver is that businesses have to go this way or they cannot survive because their pricing power will disappear.

Most people do not understand the power of this resistance. Talk about information asymmetry. Supercomputers cost more than $1 million each. These are not desktop machines; they are four orders of magnitude higher in price, and what they are capable of doing is also orders of a different magnitude. In a 2015 Microsoft commercial, for example, professor Wu Feng says, "It wasn't too long ago it would take two weeks to sequence and analyze a [single] genome; now, they do [up to] a hundred genomes per day."[17] As with other technology disruptors throughout history, this technology will destroy jobs and create new ones. It will displace some people. Those who are in the know and can harness their power will win, while those who cannot will lose.

In the early days, supercomputers were not commonly used by business— they were used by governments and academic institutions to process things like weather data to create the infamous forecast models, and they were used by university research centers. A few major corporations also used them for elite applications. The more general move into corporate business began only as big data started to be collected, new models run, and as the unrelenting price pressure of digitalization began to undercut the very ability of markets to function. Supercomputers and analytics revalue data—i.e., digits—in the capitalist system. They put prices on digits in new ways, and create priceable value. In other words, big data preserves the market mechanism regarding at least some data sets and streams.

Scaling Up a New Market

This is capitalism creating a new market. It is not finding it in geography, but rather in scale and capability. If digits are declining in value, put enough of them together and you can retain value. You can sell something that certain people will pay for. But more importantly, you can sell it to enable things that have never been done before, and that is the new market. Questions people could not previously ask, systems they could not model, data they could not understand—all these are new capabilities and they become valuable, but only in this new market.

The promise of this technology is reflected in an industry term: *predictive analytics*. Until now, data reports have always been historical. They looked backward. First you ask, *what happened?* Then probably, *why did it happen?* And perhaps, *what can we do to change it?* But it was never really feasible without supercomputers and big data to ask, *what is **going** to happen?* At first, supercomputers were used to run weather forecasting models, which are indisputably a public good. *Predictive analytics* in business is dramatically different. Rather than a public good like weather warnings, the reduction in prices of supercomputers for big data analytics has made it feasible to deploy these systems for private capital purposes.

Supercomputer-based models are being used to predict what will happen in financial markets, commodity markets, retail store markets, and so on. They are being used to predict human behavior as drivers, consumers, savers, workers, and political actors. Soon, these models will predict the actions of cancer, or the diffusion of ideas, or how videos go viral on the internet. It is not inconceivable that they will also be used to predict the behavior and actions of one's competitors.

Ultimately, the question will turn on how ubiquitous this technology can become, and whether or not it will eventually hit a limit. Recently, Sander Otte, an experimental physicist, and his team at the Delft University of Technology in the Netherlands created a nascent technology for storing digital data on a hard drive at the level of the atom. Asked about capacity, Otte said, "One estimation we made is that if you would scale this up two-dimensionally to the area of a postage stamp, that would be enough surface to keep all the books ever written by mankind."[18] He later went on to say, "for the first time in history, we are able to construct objects at a scale that was just inaccessible before."[19] If true, we are nowhere near the limit of miniaturization, and that means that technological development may have a ways to run before those limits put a stop to capitalist expansion into new, technologically created markets.

Likewise, the ubiquity of big data analytics and supercomputing power will open new markets for expansion. There is every reason to believe that hardware and software will drop in price and become increasingly available, thereby potentially creating new markets through new capabilities. To the extent that is true, this force will counteract digitalization's inexorable tendency toward a postcapitalist era. On the other hand, much of the leading software running on supercomputers is created by open source communities, thereby foreshadowing the collaborative postcapitalist communities to come. This interaction is likely to characterize the struggle between these two powerful forces for the next hundred years or more. In the end, however, society will move beyond capitalism because the intrinsic forces within make that transformation inevitable.

What About the Real Economy?

Whenever I discuss the idea of a postcapitalist economy driven by digitalization and abundance, someone inevitably asks this question: "What about real stuff? After all, not all products are digital. What about a chair, a house, or a dishwasher? You can't digitize the food we eat and the coffee we drink! Or how about this—what about the land?" Yes, of course there still needs to be the real delivery of water, real disposal of sewage, and real heat in our homes. People need these necessities, and they are not the same as, say, digital music or internet-based information.

All true, except… decreasingly so.

Here are a few facts to demonstrate what I mean:

- A chair can be 3D printed
- A dishwasher will be made of 3D printed parts and assembled by robots.
- A 3D printer can lay a concrete foundation for a home in one day.[20]
- Synthetic meat can be grown without animals.
- Shoes can be manufactured in a fully automated factory that employs no shoemakers.

Are these things "digital" yet? Not exactly, but they are headed that way. Their digital component contains more and more of the intrinsic value, and there is no stopping the growth in that value because capitalist enterprise demands such growth.

Another man asked me, "what about sales? You can't replace a salesman with a robot." Perhaps, but as a consultant in sales effectiveness, I can tell you that the industry is certainly trying. Consider these developments:

- E-commerce sites handle millions of transactions every day without human involvement.
- Artificial intelligence tracks your interests and markets products to you using offers and advertising; no person ever sells it.

- Artificial intelligence can set appointments for business-to-business sales people, thus disenfranchising the appointment setter from a job.
- Big data analytics can trace relationships between organizations to give a sales person the opportunity to find and call on the most important people in a client organization for their business.
- Sales tools track what reps are doing out in the field so methods that prove effective can be turned into best practices and taught to other reps.
- Reps frequently practice their pitches with robots, virtual reality, and/or AI feedback.

None of these replace the professional sales rep yet, but the trend is easy to see. Even sales is being overtaken by digital capabilities.

Finally, some wise guy will always ask, "What about sex?!?" You may not believe this, but today, a company called True Companion is developing a sex robot. Even the prostitution industry will be disrupted.

These examples demonstrate how digitalization is infiltrating everything.

Products are increasingly based on their one-time design, which is the digital informational component, and they are increasingly connected to the internet of things, where they receive and send information. All this information is digital.

Based on those designs and the flow of information, manufacturing systems are created that are largely robotic or digitally driven. While today factories assemble products with robots, the advent and development of 3D printing is moving manufacturing into a completely different world. Human labor is being replaced both by robots and by 3D printing, thus driving the costs of products and labor toward zero, just like it does for digital products.

Services are going to digitally driven robots as well—everything from mowing lawns, vacuuming the carpet, driverless cars, and babysitting children. It is not hard to imagine a time when products will be ordered digitally online, packed by robots, driven to your home in a driverless truck, and brought to your doorstep by a delivery robot. The only human work was placing the order, and that was done by the buyer. What is the value of labor in such a world? If there is no value to labor, who would pay for it? If you can't get paid, who would work? Labor and its compensation has been central to the capitalistic world economy—could any trend be more disruptive than this one?

Regarding our most basic necessity, nothing signifies the real economy more than food, and yet food is at the very forefront of digitalization today. We find it in the incredible power of digitalization to analyze, assess, and recreate the genetic code of plants, animals, and people. In fact, some companies are learning to manufacture food such as beef by growing beef tissue based on genetic reproduction, thereby enabling society to produce beef without cattle, pork without pigs, and chicken without the birds.

Digitalization is not just for the information economy. It's most provocative and disrupting edge occurs where digital plans are becoming more valuable than the products they create and the services robots provide. It represents a dramatic and pervasive change in our culture and economy.

The one part of the so-called real economy I have not addressed is land. Even though there are virtual digital worlds that enable people to create digital real estate and the internet provides an infinite "landmass" for the creation of sites and online spaces, these potentialities remain limited—people need a place on this earth.

Land cannot be digitalized, but it can be marginalized as a dominant factor in the productive economy. Digitalization of food and consumer products will change the way we use land, and therefore its value will change. This will change land values in agriculture, mining, forestry, and even manufacturing. Urban land used for car parking or distribution centers will also change as distribution is minimized and vehicle ownership becomes unnecessary and uncommon. Eventually, stores and retail will be obsoleted because we will be producing what we need at home on the 3D printers and similar technology. While these changes won't actually digitalize the land, they will dramatically change our relationship with it.

*

As digitalization diffuses into all corners of society and the world, human beings will still require real goods and services from the economy. Digitalization will alter nearly every possible product and service category, and as we just saw, even land will be affected. While it is true that one cannot eat digits, it is also true that everything, including what we do eat, will be increasingly produced from digitalized processes. This digital economy will deliver all that we need, but nearly all the value will be located in the digit, not the products.

II

Coping and Planning for the New Postcapitalist World

THIS SECTION OF THE BOOK EXPLORES THE possibilities of a postcapitalist society—not as science fiction, but as real possibilities emanating from the ideas, initiatives, innovations, and opportunities that are already marking the path to the future. The hope is to focus on these new directions, and to stimulate ideas, writing, and explorations by others so we may develop the thought environment necessary for building the new postcapitalist future.

Tentative Definition of Postcapitalism

The term "postcapitalism" needs definition. While it obviously points to something that comes after capitalism, it doesn't point to what the new thing is. That turn of language, however, carries a grain of essential truth. What is postcapitalism? We can say a few things. First, postcapitalism will occur during the time between capitalism and whatever comes next, but postcapitalism is what we will experience as the transition phase. Second, it is betwixt and between—a name for a time when all the old rules of capitalism are collapsing or have already collapsed, yet before the rules and practices of the new era have actually emerged. Third, postcapitalism will be an era of tremendous institutional challenges across society as this change occurs, and nothing will remain unchanged. Let's explore each of these, and then investigate some guidelines that may be helpful as we collectively and individually navigate our way through this unique period in history.

The time period associated with postcapitalism may begin with the financial meltdown of 2008-2009 which almost brought down the international finance system. But arguments could be made that it began before that as digital products and capabilities began their development. For example, the development of Web 2.0, as it was called in the early 2000s, really began the use of the internet as a practical tool for business, shopping, and social networking. Websites went beyond being the electronic brochures they had been previously when they morphed into tools for shopping, tracking sales orders, maintaining communities, training, and much more. For most people, this was when the web actually began to matter, ebooks and iTunes music came into being, and much of our contemporary digital lifestyles emerged. In other words, the apparatus, the digital products, the usefulness, and the desire to participate actually appeared on the scene, and I suspect we will look on this as the time postcapitalism really began.

Postcapitalism is betwixt and between the two eras. It will be defined by death, destruction, winding down, conflict, and endings on one hand, and emergence, birth, new paths, and unique experiences on the other. Individuals will find it very difficult to find a footing, much as people experienced in the great social, political, and religious evolutions of the past.

The difference is that these changes will be occurring *everywhere* in *every sphere* of human activity, and it will rattle us down to the very core of our understanding of work, life, and value.

The people who navigate it successfully will have an eye in both directions—they will know and understand how the old rules and structures are being affected by the postcapitalist changes, and they will also have an eye toward where things are going and be able to position themselves for the new, creative world ahead. Individuals will find, for example, that just as the sense of human and political rights becomes universal, the need for those rights will dissipate, and the claim to them will become increasingly meaningless. Likewise, many ideals of the capitalist era will come to full fruition precisely at the time they become irrelevant, and this will likely occur throughout society as the new rules and structures emerge.

At the same time, the emerging new structures will be anything but clear Like abundant nature, millions of seeds will be sown, but only a few will sprout. Success, such as it is redefined, will connect with emerging realities that stay emergent. In fact, this new world will be primarily a world of emergence in a great froth of vital rising networks and communities next to dying and marginal companies, states, and churches. The defining feature is not one or more networks that dominate, but rather that the emergence continues in an unending cycle of creativity. Human beings will require, in such a new world, a very different capacity for adaptation, a new tolerance for change, and a dedication to dealing with what is in front of them in the here and now.

Finally, postcapitalism will change everything across the board. Economics for sure, but also business, religion, social mores, sexual relations, political beliefs, and societal structures—everything that defines how human beings live, relate, and organize themselves. There have been samples of what this might feel like at different times in recent history—consider the 1960s, or the 1930s labor movement. Both were times of significant social change, but neither involved fundamental changes in the underlying economic system of how capitalism worked. Hence, they were destined not to become the dramatic, society-changing forces of postcapitalism. Postcapitalism is different. How do we know? Because capitalism itself did the same thing when it emerged five hundred years ago.

In a book called *Religion and the Rise of Capitalism,* R.H. Tawney outlines how early capitalists argued for capitalism based on religious grounds. The tenets of capitalism were said to be ordained by God in a holy order, much as the hierarchy of feudalism—especially the defense of the lords, barons, dukes, and kings—were justified based on a royal connection to God during the feudal period. In other words, the nature of the argument had not actually changed—it was still an appeal to God's will. Later, however, Tawney shows how those arguments gave way to practical arguments. As Tawney says: "After the Civil War, the attempt to maintain the theory that there was a Christian standard of economic conduct was impossible [...]."[21] But this did not occur until well into the capitalist era.

Just as the decline of feudalism was built on logic and styles of argument deriving from feudalism itself, so postcapitalism will be built on the logic and style of arguments deriving from its predecessor—capitalism. If for feudalism it was entrenched ideas of nobility that provided the argumentative basis for early capitalism, in capitalism the entrenched ideas like individual freedom, human rights, entrepreneurship, and economic liberty will underscore the arguments for the early postcapitalist era. In fact, the digitalization of nearly everything also derives its logic from capitalism, and this is why, contrary to all protest movements and social resistances, including Marxist resistance, we are now looking at the very real change and transformation of the capitalist economy. For the first time, the change is being driven by forces native to capitalism, not by outside forces that are anathema to it. Capitalism has not lost to any challengers, but it is about to lose to itself.

Capitalist Value in the Early Postcapitalist Era

My purpose in this essay is to point toward the areas of value that are likely to arise during the postcapitalist era. We know it will take a long time, we know it will be a confusing time of change, and we know that institutions will also change throughout every aspect of society—but we don't know exactly how or where because we can't completely predict the leading edge of digitalization, the limits of human acceptance or adoption of digitalization, or even the actions of those adapting or mal-adapting. There are enormous unknowns concerning the specifics, even though the general trend seems clear. Hence, what follows is my speculative assessment of where value might arise. No one really knows where all this is going, but we can make some interesting guesses for those who are looking for guidance on how to navigate the next hundred years or so.

Supercomputing & Big Data

High performance computing (HPC), also known as supercomputing, is a rising technology which capitalism may use to defend itself. It is already happening. Until the last few years, supercomputing was mostly limited to modelling complex phenomena, such as crash testing cars, engine failure in jet engines, weather models, and financial market behaviors. Supercomputers will continue to be deployed in these areas. However, increasingly, supercomputers are being used to analyze what is commonly known as big data—huge amounts of data from cell phones, email traffic, web behaviors, and the internet of things. It is a truism in technology circles today that, globally speaking, 90 percent of the currently existing data in the world was created in the last 12 months, and that fact will continue. Those amounts of data cannot actually be tended with our normal computing technologies.

In other words, supercomputers are positioned to become the processing engines of the internet of things and big data of the future. Along with them, the software to do the analysis on big data sets will be very close as well. Think of these like the people who built the shovels for the California goldminers in 1849. Here, capitalism will make a last stand against digitalization, and for the person trying to succeed within capitalism even as it crumbles, supercomputing will be a very good place to be.

Artificial Intelligence

Like big data analytics, artificial intelligence (AI) will be primed to take off on the supercomputing infrastructure as well. Although AI is limited to digitalized information, the rate of digitalization means that it will soon be able to learn just about everything. Indeed, AI is being used to analyze human behavior through changing patterns of digital behavior, and that knowledge is being applied to marketing, predictive analytics, lead generation, sports performance, and much more. Until now, processing speeds and lack of digitalization have held AI back, but as both of these develop, AI can be expected to produce amazing results for people.

Artificial intelligence can only work at least so far on digitized material or experiences, and it can only learn and develop as fast as the data can be fed to it and processed. Supercomputers provide the processing, and capitalism is driving digitalization. Because we are at its very infancy, no one knows where AI will go in the decades ahead, but it is a good bet that AI will be used first to defend capitalism, and that means value, price, and compensation for work in that area.

Solar Everything

Solar energy in particular will transform the energy component in the new economy. It is a rising technology that has been hampered by capitalistic resistance at first, and then by capitalistic takeover. The resistance occurred in the form of tax breaks to oil and gas producing companies—those companies continued the sale of oil and gas drilling leases—as well as other more subtle programs like general subsidies for shipping oil and gas on roads and through pipelines. These efforts forestalled solar energy for decades, just as capitalism would desire.

Capitalistic takeover of solar energy has occurred as the resistance capitulates. Under increasing pressure and government mandates, power-generating companies are beginning to see that they need to change. But the result is not the promotion of self-energizing and rooftop solar panels. Instead, the electric utilities are creating huge solar farms in which they mount panels across fields to collect the sun-driven power. This approach maintains the capitalist model of central investment and production, followed by distribution through a grid. The only reason to do it this way is that it maintains the capitalist structure of power generation and distribution.

An alternative model will develop because as digitalization increases, buildings will need their own source of power, as well as sources of other inputs that can be drawn from solar light, heat, and air. Today we are creating electric power from sunlight, but soon we could be producing other inputs for digitalized food production, 3D printing supplies, and similar requirements of the digitalized economy. As these things all become abundant, the logic to keeping it in a centralized location breaks down. Focal points of new value will emerge as solar power generation leaves the capitalist model and distributes generation to locations where the power is also consumed.

Networks

For most people, networks will be the hidden gem in the new digitalized economy. In the early stages, networks will be the basis of marketplace success. For decades, people have understood that their human networks drive success in work, business, and career. Some build and foster those networks better than others, and those with the best networks usually win in their marketplaces. This trend will continue in the early stages of postcapitalism people will build and maintain networks that drive capitalistic success.

But as these networks develop, their own internal logic will change them. Collaboration networks will generate free digital products because the members want to do it. People will want to participate without buying anything, and increasingly, they will become resistant to efforts to sell to them. The reason is that the value they are getting from participating in the network will far outweigh whatever widget they can buy from being it in, and the use of the network for marketing will become increasingly offensive. Eventually, they won't be valuable in the same way they were in a capitalist society.

Now, what's intriguing, however, is this: the networks themselves will be the seat of value intrinsically, and not because of the ability to sell things through them. In other words, late postcapitalism is likely to feature networks as a hallmark of postcapitalism itself, so people who are in them, influence them, lead them, create them, and manage them, are likely to be in the places where real value, satisfaction, and influence will reside. In other words, by building good networks now, you can not only maintain a strong base within capitalism in the present, you can also be well positioned for success—whatever that may mean—in the late postcapitalism period. For young people in particular, that is especially important.

Digital Information

Digitalization will shift the seat of value from the capitalist value of reproduction to the postcapitalist focus on creation. The plan will be far more important than the work. In essence, reproduction will be democratized, which means the products or creations will be available to everyone at low or no cost, but one will need digital plans to produce them.

While these plans will occupy many people and create substantial value early on—like when 3D printing becomes a useful and ubiquitous household technology—the price will also wane quickly for the same reason it did with books and music: because it is so easy to copy and reproduce at zero cost.

Performance

The one thing digitalization and the new postcapitalist world can't reproduce for free is live performance. Live performances by musicians, authors, athletes, and actors are scarce—there is only one of the performer. He or she can only be in one place at a time, and the experience of presence can't be digitally reproduced. In business, the same is true for certain kinds of training, workshop facilitations, and consulting. The physical presence of the talent or expert differentiates these experiences from those of the digital world, and presence is what these people get paid for. Musicians mostly make their living on ticket sales, not record sales. Authors become speakers. Theater and dance offer the fleeting performance as their value, and no recording will ever be the same as witnessing, spectating, participating, or being in the presence of these people.

Oddly, the value of performance will be one of the last vestiges of capitalism's primary principle—scarcity. Live performance cannot be digitalized, and that is true whether you are talking about a large-venue musical performance or a one-to-one meeting with another person. In other words, the real value will reside in one person being with another. In some cases, that will mean buying expensive tickets; in others, it will mean high-priced consulting or coaching fees; and in still others, it will simply mean the value of friendship and social camaraderie in person.

Strategies

Given these nodes of likely value, what strategies should be considered today to lay a foundation for successful navigation of the new world? Let me offer the following strategies.

First, for most people, financialization is the precursor to a postcapitalist life. Financialization, after all, means living without working—collect rents, interest payments, dividends, social security, or basic income, but no real work. The problem is that most people cannot financialize because they cannot make enough money to make it happen. The people most likely to achieve this path are the wealthy, by way of investments, and the elderly, by way of investments and social security. Everyone else needs to save and accumulate, but the chances of doing so in today's world are limited.

To that end, the young should consider doing everything possible to avoid debt, especially college debt. There may be no way to pay it back in any reasonable timeframe, or perhaps any way to pay it back at all. The alternative would say to take on all the debt you can because paying it back won't happen anyway, and if you take the debt, you will be in luck when government or circumstance eliminates it for you. This, however, would be a big gamble. While the trends are inevitable, the timeframes are unknown.

A second strategy is to focus on networks. The primary structure of value in the postcapitalist world will be networks, and people will choose their own level of involvement. Some will be as members, some as participants, some as organizers. Networks will be especially important as seats of value in the industries where digitalization is destroying the capitalistic market mechanism—books and music are obvious examples, but there will be others. Young people today are doing this in droves—much of it is social networking, but much is also social with a conscience. Young people are creating communities of common interest, advocating for social justice or religious values, or they are creating communities of interest in authors, music, issues, politics, or art. These communities, mostly online, are predominantly digital in nature. The good ones will endure through the early stages, while most will crop up, prosper, then wither and die to be replaced by something else.

In these early decades of the postcapitalist transition, many people cultivate networks through which they can raise money. Crowdfunding sources, special projects, and other work in the early decades do, in fact, need to be funded. There will come a time when the economy changes, but we are not in it now. One necessary approach is to crowdfund, and for that you need an excellent, committed network. Cultivate that—it is an important strategy.

A third strategy is to join and participate in collaborative production teams creating free products. As individuals participate in these teams, they are building the knowledge products of the future, and because those products cannot be priced, it is actually leading us into the postcapitalist future. Collaborative production teams are appearing in many guises. Many of the first are focused on software collaboration or art. At one scale, Linux, Drupal, Spark, and Hadoop are all open-sourced software systems built by teams of collaborators. On the other end, artists, musicians, and writers are operating collaboratives to work together to get their work out into the world. Thinkers and business leaders are collaborating on books, with each author contributing an essay, and then jointly publishing them, and many of these teams of authors have never met in person. Some of these collaboratives share, pool, and split funds, while others are simply contributing from a sense of passion or purpose for free. Either way, participation in this economic model will be critical to success in the future.

Fourth, career work will probably be best focused on areas that are emerging in the postcapitalist, digitalized economy. Supercomputing, artificial intelligence, and networks are obvious targets today, but a truly winning strategy will look for the new seats of value that emerge. One way to find these opportunities will be to watch industries as they digitalize. For example, I have spent 20 years as a consultant in sales effectiveness for large companies. The work is a service. I do a lot of qualitative research, facilitation, and simulations training. This world of sales effectiveness, however, is changing before my eyes. Today, my clients can use AI to digitally set sales appointments without an actual caller. They can conduct big data analytics to identify and monitor relationships between organizations. And digital sales tools for tablets enable two-way learning between the field reps and the home office, eliminating the need for about half of the research I do. In other words, my industry is changing by going digital. As a professional in contemporary business, the opportunity is in participating in the digitalization of the industry I already know. Be a part of the disruption; in this case, sell the tools. I don't need to become an app builder, but I need to make these products and services part of my business. The same is true in nearly every other industry facing digitalization.

Fifth, activities focused on the experience economy will outlast most other industries in terms of holding up value, and many people should consider this. We discussed performance previously, but the experience economy goes beyond ticketed art and sporting events. Restaurants that offer a unique experience will likely endure the early decades of the transition. Ambiance, food quality, relationships with staff—all these will matter. Distinction can be created in any of a number of ways, but the key is that it feels distinct and can only be experienced by being in a place or a space. Workers in these industries will continue to be paid wages longer than in most production industries, but for some, even that will fade as robots are waiting tables and cooking food in some new restaurants.

The sixth and final strategy I want to offer is what I call transition arbitrage. Transition arbitrage occurs in the gap between zero production cost and the eventual, but not yet here, price decrease resulting from digitalization. Many capitalists and entrepreneurs will play in this space because it is a very compelling space to be from a capitalist perspective. Cost of reproduction is falling due to digitalization, but value in the market has not changed. The market does not yet understand that the product is digitally abundant, so prices remain high. High prices and very low cost of reproduction create large profit margins—an entrepreneur's dream. When this situation can be found, a lot of money can be made.

Interestingly, the most likely place to find stubbornly high prices is in the corporate market. There is a dynamic inside companies that blinds them to these offers and makes them slow to adopt them. It has to do with standardization. As rules-based organizations, they need standards, equal treatment, and controlled processes. The early stages of a digitally abundant market are anything but orderly, and companies will pay higher prices to maintain orderliness because order is perceived to reduce risk. Small businesses that sell to these companies can deal with the orderliness problems to tremendous advantage until the market adjusts and a new pricing regimen is ubiquitous and defines the new expectation.

Several Strategies to Win

The transition to postcapitalism will create many opportunities and unrelenting change. As people position themselves in positions of value, one cardinal rule must be followed: prepare to change. Nodes of value will appear and disappear at rates never seen before, and the most dangerous position will be to imagine that one strategy will work today and forever. It won't. The idea of a single strategy working forever is a capitalist dream—the perpetual money machine that creates the money without care. It is a dangerous dream for this new world. Nothing will stay the same, and no process will work forever—maybe not even for a decade, or maybe not even for a year. The changing times ahead will result in a dramatic pace of change. Anyone not attuned to it will be left behind.

A Postcapitalist Solution to Climate Change

Scientists have known about climate change since the 1970s, when we used to refer to it as the "greenhouse effect." Now, some fifty years later, the negative effects of climate change are growing worse and more alarming every year, and no global agreement or change program has significantly tilted the balance away from catastrophe. The reason is simple: Capitalism is the cause of climate change, and nothing in the past fifty years has changed capitalism. Until now.

At this unique point in history, capitalism is terminally ill. It is not losing to government regulation, nor is it losing to socialist overthrow. Capitalism is not having a sudden fit of moral development and mending its ways. Instead, its mortal illness comes from its own intrinsic drive to cut costs and improve efficiency, which is leading to an explosion of automation and digitalization across the economy. Today, this transition is entrenched in industries like music and ebooks—industries that are being massively disrupted, but which are only at the margins of the capitalist system. It is only a matter of time before the individual disruptions of industries become a single disruption of the entire system. That disruption is the beginning of postcapitalism—and the solution to climate change.

The Emerging Postcapitalist Era

Why can we be confident that a postcapitalist era is emerging? Here are four key factors leading us into a postcapitalist future:

- First, everything is becoming increasingly digital. Industrial production systems, electric grids, consumer products, ebooks, and even driverless cars. The digits and their digital products come from sensors and internal computers, connect over the internet of things, and gain meaning through analytics. *Everything* is getting a larger and larger digital component.
- Second, as individual products become increasingly digitalized, their prices will trend rapidly toward zero. In digits, there is no marginal

cost to reproduction, and therefore no floor on price. As a result, capitalist competition will drive prices toward zero.

- Third, while capitalism is based on the notion of scarcity, a postcapitalist economy will be based on abundance. Digitalization creates a cost-free, infinite supply, but markets cannot function in a world of abundance because infinite supply makes it impossible to set prices.
- Fourth, if you have a world in which goods cannot be priced, it is also impossible to price labor. If labor can't earn income, consumers cannot buy. When consumers stop buying, the economy stops working.

These four factors seem likely to arise in any postcapitalist world mainly because they derive from the logic of capitalism itself. The drive to reduce costs, the competition between producers, and the reliance on consumer purchasing power are all central to capitalism, so capitalism will not resist these changes. Outside forces, such as regulation and revolution, cannot stop it—a fact proven over centuries of outside critique. The forces driving the emergence of a postcapitalist era are intrinsic and unavoidable, and therefore inevitable.

How can postcapitalism help solve climate change?

As the postcapitalist era emerges, it will develop the principles, structures, and methods that will constitute *its own* internal logic. The seeds of that logic are laid in the factors just described, but how they might develop is a matter of speculation, imagination, and possibility. We can see examples of how that logic may play out, and its impact on climate change, in five illustrative areas: networks, energy, the free economy, food, and transportation.

Networks

The dominant organizational structure of postcapitalism is the network—not corporations, markets, or government. Those three, after all, are the three legged stool on which capitalism stands. Networks represent discontinuity. They are not states and they are not governments. They are not corporations, and they are not markets. They are something novel. People contribute to them because they want to, not because they get paid. There are many kinds of networks—those for creating valuable products like Wikipedia, those that are social, those that foster collaboration, and those that enable trade. These examples are content-centered networks, but there are also the physical networks—Facebook, Twitter, Comcast, and SaaS online networks. These networks provide the actual *mechanism* by which the other networks function. Finally, there remain people-to-people networks that are not primarily about digits, but which now have an additional glue to hold them together. These are professional networks, in-person conferences, etc.—all of which are enabled and magnified by digital networks.

Subversive to political and organizational boundaries, networks spread across national borders as if those borders do not exist. They spread across corporate boundaries, blurring the lines between us and them, and confounding competition. In my work as a consultant, I find that more and more corporate people find their professional, career-advancing networks not within their corporate walls, but rather within the links and connections they make and maintain every day with other professionals in their area of work. Indeed, those connections are often viewed as far more enduring, important, and valuable than the connections they make within their companies. When they are looking for solutions to problems, they don't talk to their bosses, they talk to their professional colleagues in their network, most of whom work in other companies.

Networks, like climate change, are global in nature. Where nations and churches inherently fail at global solutions, digital networks are unrestricted and global by default. They connect people globally irrespective of national boundaries, and they will enable the collaboration needed to solve the climate change problem.

Abundant Power

Oil is oil, and while it is not digital, the industry increasingly relies on digital insights and information to find oil, drill for it, process it, ship it, and burn it. As a product of the real economy, oil will always be scarce—if people stop drilling for it, it will become scarce and that makes it subject to market pricing.

On the other hand, sunlight is abundant, and solar power is essentially digital in and of itself. Solar power operates very similarly to digital products. Once you can get that sunlight converted into power, the next batch of power has almost no marginal cost to produce. The only cost tracked to marginal cost of production is depreciation of the equipment, but as the equipment may last a very long time, the marginal cost trends toward zero. As the price for that equipment drops because of automation and digitalization, the marginal cost goes down even further. In other words, solar power operates in a postcapitalist fashion. This is one reason it has been so ardently opposed by capitalist enterprises. It is subversive to the very economy of capitalism.

In the early stages of the postcapitalist economy, adoption will depend on pricing mechanisms, but solar power generation has so far gone in two interesting and opposite directions. In the first, capital-driven power generators, such as utilities, have tried to control it through a capitalist model, and they have been supported in this effort with state subsidies. Instead of providing free and independent energy sources, these utilities have begun to create huge solar farms covering big spans of earth. These solar farms are large, remote production facilities which then send the power over the grid to where people and businesses use it—just like the oil, coal, and nuclear power generation model used since the 1800s. These capital-driven companies are preserving the producer/consumer dichotomy inherent to capitalism. That system enables the power company to control access, restrict availability, and thereby create scarcity and restrict abundance. While better in many ways than burning fossil fuel, it is a capitalist attempt to preserve the market in energy, which is no longer needed.

The converse program is playing out in companies like Wal-Mart, which have installed solar panels on their rooftops as a cost-cutting measure. Wal-Mart generates the power on its own premises, uses the power, and may even sell some to the power company over the grid. If you think of this as a model, the producer/consumer dichotomy is dissolved, and companies or homes adopting the same approach are essentially replacing that capitalist construct with a postcapitalist model. There is no need for large producers or solar farms anymore. Rather, power will be generated from the rooftops of homes and businesses for their own consumption. Digital systems will control and manage the power for the building or operation; thus, the kind of heavy capital investment found in traditional power generation will become an anachronistic model of the past.

Solar power, like digitalization, is a key driver of the postcapitalist economy. If we are able to build and embrace this sooner, perhaps with government help, we may be able to stave off the more extreme effects of climate change. If not, these changes will come later, but only after enormous human suffering.

Free Economy

The abundant postcapitalist society will lead to an economy in which most things are free. As products or services become abundant or digitalized, markets will cease to function, and prices will collapse. This will be the ultimate cause of the undoing of capitalism. What does that mean?

If digital products are abundant and have no cost, then the products cannot be priced, and neither can the labor to produce them. If labor cannot be priced, no one gets paid for working and demand disappears. In this situation, money doesn't just lose value, it ceases to matter because most things we will need are free. With that, whole new possibilities occur.

Imagine, for example, what a free, cashless economy would mean. It will engender the development of non-capitalistic lifestyles in which work and consumption—two pillars of capitalist economy—no longer rule our economic lives. With no financial requirement to go to work, commuting is no longer necessary or economical. With home-based, digital production of nearly everything, there is no need to distribute or transport goods. Energy is free from the sun, as we saw in the previous section, so everything we do to burn stuff is unnecessary. In essence, the forced burning of scarce, extracted resources comes to an end—hence, a *real* solution to climate change.

Food

Digitalization is likely to push us even further into areas once thought impossible. One would think that food, for example, is not an area where digitalization would become a component of price. Yet today, private companies are developing ways of growing the tissues for our food without the animal. Using stem cells, genetic information and specialized, scientific feeding processes, these companies aim to "grow a steak" without growing a cow. Same with chicken, pork, and other meats, as well as fruits and vegetables. Should this become an accepted way of producing food, it could be said that food, at that point, is largely digitalized. You grow it not based on animals and acres of land, but rather based on a digital genetic code and a feedstock of some sort—much of which will include digitalized solar energy. This could be done centrally and distributed through digital delivery—driverless cars or drones, for example—or perhaps set up in homes to create your own food. As long as there is a need for a non-digital feedstock, some marginal cost of production will be maintained. But it will be far less than the capitalist costs associated with current animal production and distribution.

Although many readers (including me) will be horrified by the idea of digitalized food, it will be a part of the postcapitalist world, and as such, it will actually contribute to solving climate change. As digital food becomes more common, none of the existing industrialized agricultural infrastructure will survive—not the tractors, not the million-chicken egg houses, not the 10,000 head cow barns, and not the giant plains feedlots. The processing plants will disappear or intensively localize, and the distribution networks will no longer be needed. All industrial agriculture contributes to climate change, and the whole system will disappear with the rise of "digital food."

Transportation

The decreasing importance (i.e. value) of the automobile is evident in a little-recognized trend in teenage behavior. Back in the 1970s and 1980s, the single most important teenage right of passage was obtaining one's driver's license. Being able to drive provided independence and not only the keys to the car, but the keys to the world. Almost everyone took the test on their 16th birthday. Here's what's different: more and more of today's teenagers couldn't care less about driving. It's not uncommon for teens to not bother with driving until after they turn 18 or even 20 years old. Why? Because "getting somewhere" is no longer nearly as important socially as "being online." The mobility provided by cars is no longer critical to one's social standing, which is pretty much how teens measure everything, but *digital access* is. By 18, 20, or older, these same kids need a car to get to work—in other words, they want to drive only when there is an economic value to getting somewhere. When that economic value is no longer pertinent, the allure of the automobile is likely to wane considerably, just as it did for teens who increasingly find driving irrelevant.

If you analyze the way most people use cars today, it is apparent that the value they derive from their cars is rooted in meeting three primary needs—getting to and from work, getting to a from the places they need to procure things, and getting to and from other people. Practically speaking, that's it. Some will also buy cars for image purposes, but even that is usually tied to work or social status. Cars add value through work, procurement of goods, and social access.

As the digitalized economy loses the power to price work, the price one is willing to pay for a car changes. Who needs to buy a car to get to work if work doesn't pay? Likewise, if a person can begin to procure the goods needed to live effectively and efficiently without a car, what price is one willing to pay for the procurement component of the car's value? Add that to the teen's assessment that cars don't matter for sociability, and there is little left to support the economics of car buying.

Conversely, as driverless vehicles become ubiquitous, we are likely to summon a car when we need it. There is no need to own them, park them, or insure them. Instead, electricity will power the car based on solar energy production, thereby eliminating the single largest component of a pollution creating climate change—automobile emissions.

The Climate Change Solution

As long as we have capitalism, climate change will be an intransigent problem. We know what is causing it—extractive energy programs, massive burning of fuel for transportation and energy, hierarchical organization, growing feedlots, and the intrinsic need to price and pay for everything. In short, the cause of climate change is capitalism. Hence, we will defeat climate change only when capitalism ceases to dominate the global economic, political, and social system.

The good news is that capitalism's own intrinsic logic is taking us toward a postcapitalist world in which new energy, transportation, and food production methods dominate, networks re-organize society, and the free economy creates an unprecedented experience of abundance—thereby undermining the core principles of capitalism. This transition is upon us, but it will be a long time before it takes hold. It should be our hope and our work that postcapitalism arises before climate change becomes both catastrophic and irreversible.

Abundant Digital Food

To the extent that digitalization is the primary driver behind the emergence of a postcapitalist economy, one question nearly always bubbles to the top in casual conversation: what about food? It's a good question. Of all things we humans need, food is among the most critical. It is also among the most complicated to secure. All of our food begins as a living organism, then it must be harvested, sent to distribution points, possibly processed, distributed again, purchased in a store, and finally get to our tables in various states of freshness to be edible and healthy.

This complicated economic problem of feeding people has given rise to an enormous food infrastructure that includes farms, processing plants, packaging and shipping, grocery stores and food co-ops, the kitchen in a home, and the waste treatment process in sewage systems, compost, and waste hauling. It includes mining and distribution of minerals, processing and delivering chemicals for fertilizer and pesticides, and the production of huge, powerful farm machinery. Of all commodities, food's origin in living organisms seems to suggest it could never be produced with digital abundance. I thought the same thing, but new advances on the frontiers of science are changing that and may lead directly to digital food abundance.

Digital food is different from other digital products for one simple reason—it is alive. Food products must be grown, fed, and nourished, and the wastes removed and dealt with. Truth be told, the earth itself is exquisitely good at this. Indeed, its natural abundance is so substantial that it can support the billions of people on this planet, plus all the other living organisms. Unfortunately, all these systems are under severe ecological stress due primarily to the extractive aspect of capitalism, but so far, we are still producing enough food to feed the world.

As two areas of leading research come to fruition, they are likely to play significant parts in an abundant, digital food world. First, the rise of animal-less or "cultured" meat is setting the table for a fully digitalized method of producing meat. Companies today are growing meat in laboratories based on harvested stem cells. In fact, in February 2016, Memphis Meats announced the creation of its first animal-less meatball.[22] Other companies like Modern Meadow in New York and Mosa Meat in Europe are doing the same thing. In fact, according to FactCoExist.com, "In 2013, with the backing of Google co-founder Sergey Brin, Mosa Meat founder Mark Post held a taste test of the world's first cultured hamburger."[23]

The technology is based on stem cells. Producers harvest the stem cells from the animal, then culture them in a lab, and a machine grows the muscle tissue needed without ever having an animal. This way of creating food will create a massive disruption in the agriculture industry, which is perhaps the single most capital intensive industry in the world. Even if there is no directly digital component, the stem-cell driven disruption to capitalism will be enormous.

The second key technology is the processing system for growing these living tissues. No doubt the first systems will simply be an enclosed system in which the culturing process adds nutrients for the cells to grow and captures waste to dispose of it. The early machines will require expensive purchased inputs, but it won't stay that way.

Why can I say that with confidence? Look what is happening in hydroponics and new food production systems. Hydroponics is essentially the same concept as the meatless beef—plants are grown for human consumption in the most artificial way—with no soil, with roots growing in nutrient-rich water, indoors, under artificial light. Hydroponics has been around for several decades. What's interesting isn't the fact of hydroponic growing enterprises, but rather how they are being combined with other growing systems. For example, James Prokopanko the former CEO of Mosiac, the world largest producer of potash and phosphate as fertilizers for agriculture, shared in a presentation at the University of Minnesota in April 2016 that hydroponic producers are joining their systems to other farming methods, such as fish farming. In this interesting system, the waste from the fish is filtered through the hydroponic system, thereby providing the necessary nutrients for the hydroponic plants. Likewise, the old and dead plants are provided as food to the fish. Other than the energy input of heat and light, this little system is moving rapidly toward a no input, no output production system.[24] It is not too difficult to imagine that you could replace the fish farm with a cultured meat system.

Today, the production of cultured meat begins with harvested stem cells, but it doesn't seem too hard to believe that the industry will soon begin with a genomic sequence instead—purely digital information from which to start the production of a steak or chicken breast. Start with the digital sequence, add the proper energy, provide the necessary conditions, and things start to grow. In other words, the digital component of the product is increasingly dominant, and that will be the part that has no marginal cost of production.

The ongoing march of technology is likely to drive digitalization into the food system in unforeseen ways. For example, we could anticipate miniaturization of these systems to culture meats—so much so, that it may one day be possible to grow your own meats in your own home by selecting digital recipes—essentially the genome for a T-bone steak. The inputs may arise from the waste from an affiliated system, or perhaps they only exist as energy generated from an abundance of sunshine. It is entirely possible that food could be produced for free and in totally abundant supply all throughout the world.

Of course this is all speculative, but research and development are already addressing this area. Food is probably the hardest and most difficult category to digitalize toward abundance, but like all other forms of digitalization, capitalism will drive us there because it is compelled to by its own cost-reduction logic. The real marker for entering true postcapitalism will occur when food is digital, totally abundant and the price is free. Such food will be very different from how we think of "organic" food today, but abundant food, produced at the level of the home, promises compelling benefits—we could end world hunger, dismantle capitalism, and provide people with a new kind of independence. The trade-offs will not be perfect, but they will be compelling, and we are better off to begin thinking about this now.

Postcapitalist Possibilities in the Subscription Economy

Most current commentaries on digitalization and automation from a postcapitalist point of view are overly negative in their connotations and seemingly desperate in their recommended solutions. Millions of people will lose their jobs, markets will fail catastrophically, and basic income is the only answer. Whether you anticipate these outcomes or not, they certainly neglect a more positive outlook emanating from the entrepreneurial software industry where digitalization is a way of life. In that industry, they combined a product with internet-based access, and called it a subscription. Instead of owning the software, users lease access to it through a license and utilize the product via the internet. This solution presents enormous opportunities today, yet for the long term, it could also usurp the greatest potential of postcapitalism and become a new foundation for the wealthy one percent to project power.

Digital Subscriptions as a Business Model

It is no accident that the subscription model arose in the software industry—software is inherently digital. Digital products, like books, software, and music, have zero marginal cost to reproduce and infinite supply, so they tend to move the price toward zero in a market economy. Software makers realized this when their software started getting "pirated" from their perspective, and free copies began to circulate. Developing the products was expensive and time consuming but with zero cost of reproduction, the industry could not support a price with a margin. They needed another solution, and that's when subscriptions became more common. Subscriptions provide a way to price these products, especially when you have free distribution and access provided via the internet. Today, the model is becoming so common that new names for them are emerging—memberships, continuity programs, access fees, and most common, software-as-a-service (SaaS). The model a company selects tends to depend on the type of digital product they are selling. There are at least two kinds of digital products: *static products* and *developing products*.

Static Products

Static products are created once, enjoyed repeatedly, and can be reproduced at zero cost. The best example of this is recorded music, however e-books, digital tools and templates, and similar products fall into this category as well. Static products provide a clear example of how digitalization eliminates the cost of production.

But let's be clear about this category; we are not just talking about music and books. As more and more static products become digitalized, their prices will also drive toward zero since they have little or no marginal cost for reproduction. It starts with books and music, but as products are more commonly manufactured from 3D printing, for example, the largest single component of the cost and work of creating the product will be the plan that drives the 3D printer—much as the single biggest cost of creating a book or piece of music today is the creative work of the artist. After that initial creation, it costs nothing, or nearly nothing, to reproduce the final product, and that's why prices head toward zero.

Developing Products

The other category, *developing products,* are qualitatively different from static products. *Developing products* change, improve, and revise over time—in short, they *develop*. Customers buy the product, but they also buy the stream of developments and improvements which change the product over time. This dynamic is only possible with digital products.

In the early days of software sales, the capitalist paradigm began with the assertion of intellectual property rights, and the buyer was to purchase a finished product, much as a car is a finished product. You get your disks, put them into your computer, and once the files all load, you are good to go. Except there was a problem. The rapid advances in software, as well as the problems of bugs, viruses, and other challenges, meant that the development process continued after the sale, and it was actually never in a completely finished state. Companies such as Microsoft tried to get all customers to register so they could send them updates to the software, or they included a maintenance contract in the deal. Now, most software doesn't even provide a disk anymore; instead, you download the product onto a machine and the manufacturer automatically updates it for you. You simply pay for the product via subscription, and if you don't make your payment, they automatically disable the product on your computer.

Business Impact

Although the subscription model protects price in the short term, prices will still tend toward zero. Google Office software, for example, is achieving increasing use among young companies, millennials, and entrepreneurs, and larger firms will begin to adopt these kinds of tools as trust is built. Google Office is free. It is not the same as Microsoft Office, but it is close; many of the features most people need or use in MS Office are in Google Docs, for example. The reason is that even in the cloud—indeed, perhaps especially in the cloud—the marginal cost of reproduction is zero. People are just using what is there. The only real marginal cost is the cost of memory, and that has been rapidly declining toward zero as well—especially for every day applications.

The subscription model also developed tools created for people to use on the internet. Commonly called SaaS models (software-as-a-service), these business models are oriented to allow people access to an online tool where they can do work, store their data or information, and collaborate effectively. The big business names in this space include Salesforce.com, Dropbox, iCloud, Basecamp, and Marketo. For consumers, most mobile apps fall into this category. Many others are coming, and others still are converting to SaaS models.

The value of these models lies not in the software itself, but in the ability to accept, process, organize, and represent data that is important to businesses primarily. But here, there is a long-term convergence. Business-based SaaS systems are becoming increasingly similar in their functionality. They will highlight particular features for particular needs, but they are all adding contact databases, CRM-like services, reporting, emailing, and other similar functions. Whether it is volunteer management for large companies, CRM systems for sales organizations, or high-security document sharing, the systems are converging in terms of what they do. CRM systems add financial forecasting, and financial bookkeeping includes contact databases. Automated marketing systems can email customers, but so can Salesforce.com and your financial software. Differentiation is based increasingly on new innovations at the margins, but the core of business SaaS systems is that they are all becoming more and more similar to one another. Hence, in this market, you have decreasing differentiation and a vanishing marginal cost working together, and the results are the same—reduced cost and price. The price of the core of these systems moves toward zero, again because there is no marginal cost to adding users. It also moves toward zero because of the lack of differentiation. Both forces are at work in this area.

External Forces

So far, we have only addressed those dynamics inherent to the company itself, and it can be assumed that a business will not run itself out of business by charging nothing. While that is true, other people will and do charge nothing. For every type of business system, you can find an online collaboration that is producing the same product as a collaborative community and offering it to others at zero cost. Hence, Linux undermines Windows, Sugar CRM undermines Salesforce.com, and Wordpress undermines website builders. Entire communities of people willing to work for free do so to create shareware and freeware simply because they can. Once done, there is no incremental cost, and many of these people are simply fascinated with the possibility of doing so. This is digital logic at play, and while you can stay ahead for a while, there is virtually no way to compete capitalistically with comparable products that are free or have no price.

The Opportunity Now

While the long term trend will continue to challenge a subscription business model, there remain many opportunities to sustain profitability using subscriptions, and some are better for business, while others are better for consumers.

Consumer

In consumer software, most subscriptions are now an annual payment to subscribe for the year, much like a magazine. The value of a tool needs to continually prove its worth, but if it is there, customers renew and cash flows. Companies usually sell the subscription on the basis of a monthly cost, but they charge annually and that is how most people buy them.

The consumer market, however, also responds to the smaller, more incremental monthly payment method. Adobe sells some of its creative products like Photoshop for $10 per month. People make small monthly payments to other online services for things like video rental (Netflix and Amazon), video storage and streaming (AudioAcrobat), and file management and sharing (Dropbox.com). These purely digital products are obvious, but similar models are extending into other online businesses where distribution is free, or you become a member of a web community for $1-3 per month.

Business

Business software is also sold on subscription, but at higher price points and usually in bundles. Some of these services can be elaborate and very expensive, such as legal research services, for example, which can cost an attorney hundreds or even thousands of dollars per month, or CRM systems which can be hundreds of dollars or more per person per year. Businesses will access new management tools, and the independent solo entrepreneur can develop his or her own online presence which, when people value it, they subscribe to support and maintain it. The opportunity lies in the actual access to entire global digitalized market, and the fact that it can be reached by one person working alone or by a large business, and the product/service can be monetized.

The point is that the buyer accesses the software via subscription, not purchase. Subscription is a leading practice for businesses today. While it may seem brilliant, the sole reason is that digital products cannot be sold at market the way they are supposed to in capitalism. People are moving to subscription because the market model has been disrupted.

The Risks and Challenges

Although the subscription economy provides opportunity to many people as we transition toward postcapitalism, it is not without its risks. Such an economy presupposes an expanded regimen of intellectual property—the products are owned by their makers, and people buy access, not products. Products purchased in this manner are transient. They disappear as soon as we stop paying. Hence, control of the most important assets is concentrated even further, thereby enriching the top 1% with tremendous wealth. Yet for society, the underlying structure moves us not toward a hopeful postcapitalism, but rather into a *financialized rentism*,[25] in which the wealthy, the corporate, and the creative own the digital property, and everyone else is a renter.

In addition, this model is profoundly dependent upon a free and open internet, something its proponents rarely acknowledge or even strategize upon. Low cost for internet access and equal delivery of everyone's content is essential to this system. Unfortunately, the private companies that provide cable, DSL, and satellite internet access have no interest in keeping prices down or ensuring all content has access. They seek to charge more for preferred content providers to make sure their content is delivered quickly, and they seek the highest fees they can charge.

This bias against the free and open internet produces two concerns. First, people who are building subscription economy products assume that the internet will operate as a utility and all content will be delivered fairly, and that there will not be any upcharges in order to keep their customers happy with fast access to their products. Instead, they assume that service will remain, essentially, free to them. Should that stop being the case, the subscription business model will be dramatically slowed in its development, and may even collapse.

Second, this bias provides the private companies who own the networks a stranglehold over the digital economy of the world, and thereby a foothold by which capitalism may still project its power. Similar to the railroads of the 1850s, the steel mills of the early 1900s, and the phone and car companies of the 20th century, these companies are positioned to determine winners and losers by way of their sheer scale, utility and essentiality to the digital economy. They will not stop the emergence of digitalized postcapitalism, but they may slow it down. Since the financial crisis of 2008-2009, "too big to fail" has described certain banking and financial institutions, yet the same could be said of the cable, satellite, and DSL internet companies. Some in society will inevitably ask when these institutions cease to be private enterprises and need to be treated like regulated public utilities.

The Way Forward

Despite these risks, the subscription business model appears to be here to stay, and it will likely serve the interests of digital entrepreneurs of all sizes and shapes. Indeed, it presents the opportunity for people living through this transition to prosper, even as the capitalist system declines. The subscription economy is a bridge economy, and so long as we think of it that way, it will serve its participants well. Everyone else becomes a temporary renter, but the key term is *temporary*—we will soon transition to a different economy altogether.

Problems and Opportunities with the Universal Basic Income Dream

What if you had enough income to live on and never had to work another day in your life? That, in essence, is the promise of universal basic income (UBI). Government gives everyone cash with no strings attached. It is an old idea with a new application. Decades ago, libertarians and socialists championed the idea, and during the Nixon administration, the United States almost passed it. Today, the idea has been given new life as one answer to the biggest problem we face as digitalization destroys jobs—how will people buy things? The UBI answer: simply give everyone enough money to live on. They can still work if they can find a job, but they don't have to work to stay out of poverty.

Support for the idea is coming from all quarters. Libertarians support it as a much easier and simpler way to alleviate poverty and shrink the federal bureaucracy at the same time. Socialists and progressives support it because of its effect on poverty and the view that UBI can unleash new forms of creativity among the public. Labor leader Andy Stern, the former head of SEIU, supports it in his newest book *Raising the Floor*, as a way of addressing new joblessness among working people. Even leading capitalist investors like bond king Bill Gross see basic income as a new reality, and one that will be good and necessary for the economy.[26]

The UBI Concept

UBI is easy enough to grasp conceptually. The government simply gives people money without regard to work. In the United States, one idea gives $1,000 per month to every adult in the country. Married people net $24,000 per year from the government. Although not quite middle class, the amount is enough to keep people above the poverty line.[27] Bolder proposals would give more money to help ensure people can be in the middle class.

For those of us conditioned in capitalist morality, this idea is an abomination. Give everyone something for nothing? No way! We'd create a nation of sloth! Everyone would quit working, and then what would we do? Yet the idea has come to the fore again as the world stares down a juggernaut that is going to prevent most people from working anyway. Digitalization, roboticization, automation, and artificial intelligence are going to replace most jobs. While this is easy to see, the consequences of such a change are not.

As many have asked, what are all these people going to do when their jobs are automated or roboticized? How will they occupy their time? How will they obtain money, food, and the necessities of life? How will they keep their homes? The challenge is that there are likely to be millions of these people without jobs in a relatively short period of time. Right now, the lowest wage jobs in the world are being replaced with robots. Bangladeshis are losing their jobs because shoemakers like Adidas are moving production closer to market and replacing people with robots.[28] More and more manufacturing is being replaced by robots, but so are service jobs of all kinds. Here are a few highlights:

- Financial services firms are using AI to write stock analyses and reports[29]
- Retail companies are testing robotic greeters
- Fast food is deploying robots to build hamburgers
- 3D printers are manufacturing all kinds of parts
- Driverless cars will soon be eliminating taxi and Uber drivers, and driverless trucks—which are already being used in mines—will be delivering freight[30]
- Hospitals are using robotic bins to move everything from pharmaceuticals to laundry around the hospital

The applications go on and on. The only job category that is immune requires the physical presence of a human being—think of musical performances, mental health therapy, or sporting events. The point is to be with the person you are with because of what they provide as an experience for you—and no robot will replace that. Beyond this category, it is hard to see a category that is safe from automation and robotics.

A Solution: Universal Basic Income

Basic income is being touted as the answer to this problem, and in the short run, it probably is. UBI provides cash so that people can meet their basic needs. With enough income to provide basic needs, work is a choice rather than an existential coercion. People would be free to create and grow businesses without the threat of homelessness, but they'd also be free to choose to do nothing. As a society we would need to accept this reality.

On the other hand, if the jobs do not disappear all at the same time, the $24,000 per married couple could dramatically increase purchasing power. It would function at the family level like a $24,000 per year raise—that much more money for spending, saving, investing, or purchasing durable goods. Economic growth would take off because, unlike in tax cuts, most of the money goes to people who will spend it.

If UBI does not come into being as the transition to a postcapitalist future occurs, there are some unattractive alternatives. One possibility is enormous swelling of the social safety programs currently in place—the precursor of which we have already seen in the substantial growth of social security disability benefits since the 2008 financial crisis. Most of the jobs lost during that crisis have not returned, so people have turned to the only program available. Many will get a doctor to say they cannot work, and they qualify for benefits. Disability benefits are only one part of the social safety net; we can expect many others to grow as well, should we decide to work only with the traditional programs.

Another alternative would be economic collapse and the casting of millions of middle class Americans into poverty. While this idea may be ideologically pure to those who felt there should be no intervention to solve the financial crisis back in 2008, it has a moral repugnance that most people find objectionable. We don't want to see millions of people in poverty, empty grocery store shelves, and general economic malaise. America can do better, we think to ourselves, and we should.

Challenges with Universal Basic Income

Basic income, however, raises many intriguing questions. First, why should basic income be so minimal? Twenty-four thousand dollars per year may keep a couple barely above the poverty line, but it will hardly stave off economic collapse. The consumption power of $24,000 is nowhere near the 2015 median income of more than $56,000.[31] If a large number of people move from an income of $56,000 to $24,000, you can expect the GDP to take an enormous hit. Seventy percent of our economy is based on consumer purchasing—clothing, cars, restaurant meals, building supplies, and all the other things people do with their money. On $24,000 a year, nearly all of that purchasing power disappears. Sure, people have food and shelter, but that's it. A massive shift to income levels at 50 percent of the previous is not a recipe for prosperity, even though it may buy us some time.

If we are to have a UBI, we should take out the term "basic." We don't need a minimal income, we need an income that can support a thriving economy. I propose that it should be equal to the median income in the country, thereby lifting people into a lifestyle that can support the economic vitality of the nation. At least, that is, until digitalism drives prices down to zero, at which time hardly any income will be needed anyway. Basic income should bridge the gap.

Another reason basic income should be more than basic refers to a common argument for UBI—the unleashing of creativity through art, business, and entertainment. UBI is supposed to give people time for other pursuits if they can't find a job. If there are no jobs and the income allows for no extras, however, who will buy the art, who will buy from the new business, and who will buy the tickets for entertainment? Without enough income, you cannot create economic vitality.

Herein, however, a second problem occurs. If there is basic income, the consumption economy of capitalism is supported. This is why traditionally conservative people like investors and economists support basic income—they can see that without it, purchasing power will drop, and when people stop spending, capitalism is in trouble. These people have an instinct for wealth preservation, and that instinct is opening their eyes to the challenges we soon face.

Do we want to perpetuate capitalism? Especially if there is an alternative? Unless you are particularly wealthy, the only reason to preserve capitalism is to avoid economic shock. But the shock is coming anyway. Jobs are being cut and lost slowly right now, but in the next 20 years, an enormous number of jobs of all kinds will disappear.

The avoidance of the economic shock, however, is a worthy purpose. It will soften the blow for millions of people whether they are employed or not. It will perpetuate some jobs for a longer period of time. It will enable ongoing spending, as well as the purchase of homes. Basic income at a high enough level will actually preserve wealth for a longer period of time while the free economy aspect of digitalization catches up. That development is likely to be more gradual and less impactful than the mass loss of jobs, so our economic lives can withstand it.

That said, basic income will require an end date as a policy. While a catastrophic collapse of the consumer economy would hurt everyone, the perpetuation of extraction capitalism will too because it will continue to drive climate change. Basic income can be used as a way to avoid changing the paradigm. While that is good in the short run as a cushion, in the long run it is disastrous, and may lead us into exogenous shocks that historically accompany dramatic shifts in socioeconomic systems.

We have a choice. We can refuse basic income and instigate an economic disaster, or we can create basic income and court a climatic disaster. We can only win by properly managing basic income, and climate policy at the same time. While this duality seems daunting, they can actually work together. Once we establish UBI, there is far less power in any argument against dealing with climate change that is bases on saving jobs. UBI, which is created to address job loss, is already in place. Since jobs are no longer necessary for survival, the speciousness of the argument is even more evident.

Managing Basic Income

The primary allure of basic income to libertarians is the elimination of the federal bureaucracy managing the social safety net. Libertarians think, "Well, the government is good at cutting checks, so let's just have it do what it is good at and cut checks to everyone. The 136 programs that are currently charged with giving welfare and social safety net money to people who qualify—that is, to only the right people in the right circumstances—can be eliminated."[v] Nice idea, but not so fast. There is probably a lot to be gained, but let's consider the challenges.

The first challenge is definition: how much is a basic income? Rent, food, and other costs of living are so different across the country that setting a number would be impossible. Take any number and the differences could be striking. What might allow you to live like a king in rural Mississippi might not even cover your rent in New York City. How would basic income address these geographic differences in economic need for a basic standard of living? And if you did account for them, how do you change the income

---

[v] ghgh

level when a person moves? Perhaps a little more management of the program is required than initially thought.

The second challenge is how to pay for it. Andy Stern in his book *Raising the Floor* provides what he calls a menu of options for funding a very basic UBI. Here are the sources he lists and the possible annual revenue:

- Eliminating the 126 currently existing welfare programs: $1 trillion
- Eliminating the federal government's tax expenditures: $1.2 trillion
- VAT tax of 5-10 percent: $650 billion to $1.3 trillion
- Financial Transaction Tax: $150 billion
- User fees for natural resources: $1.25 trillion
- Wealth tax of 1.5 percent: $600 billion
- Expenditure changes in the budget: $100 billion[32]

Stern estimates that his program would cost up to $2.5 trillion, so he concludes that the money is there.

A far more promising approach is to tax the work of robots, AI, and other means of production that are replacing salaries. Bill Gates and others have suggested this route, and it is very reasonable. Measuring work to get the tax right would be a challenge, but that is achievable. This strategy also must align with the actual number of jobs eliminated, so it can scale accordingly.

In my estimation, Stern's approach would be a starting point, and the robot/automation tax would slowly replace all the other taxes that support UBI. This replacement would occur gradually as robots are integrated into the economy. Such a hybrid approach could be excellent long term policy and create appropriate benefits for everyone—capitalists get their automation, workers get the money they need to live on, government gets the funds to keep governing.

A couple of other options are also worth considering, especially if we are thinking about moving to the larger basic income that Stern proposes. One is to tax corporate dividends, interest, and rent the way we do other income, and eliminate the ceiling on income subject to social security tax. Corporate profits are earned by virtue of the privileges granted to corporations by the people—from the right to organize as a corporation to low prices for extraction leases to the every-so-many-decades bail outs we fund through borrowing and public debt. Just the companies on the S&P 500 payout more than one trillion dollars per year in dividends, and most of the dividends go to wealthy stockholders. These dividends receive special treatment in taxes—they are exempt from payroll taxes because they are thought to be "unearned" income. Total housing rents in the United States amount to $440 billion according to Zillow.[33] Payroll dollars not subject to FICA tax are estimated at about $1 trillion. Suffice it to say that somewhere in the neighborhood of $3-5 trillion could be taxed at the FICA rate, and if so, would raise $350-600 billion in revenue.

Yet another option to consider takes the whole thing off the books, just like they did when they bailed out the banks—by creating a quantitative easing type of program. Instead of being on the national budget where legislators had to agree, the Federal Reserve started buying bonds with money it did not have—to the tune of about $80 billion per month (or $1 trillion dollars per year).[34] The idea was to provide "liquidity" in the markets by removing so-called toxic debt, and to prop up the economy by providing stimulus. As jobs disappear under the coming wave of digitalization, we will face the same kind of crisis. Since people will not be able to pay their bills, debt will turn toxic. Since people will have no salary, they won't be able to buy. This time when it happens, let's take a different approach. The Federal Reserve can inject liquidity by enabling the people who cannot be employed any more to pay their bills. It can invent money it doesn't have to again create stimulus. If it could do this for several years adding trillions of dollars to the economy through banks, how about doing it with real people? One way or another, they can play a role in making this happen.

Many options exist for funding UBI, and the argument that there is no way to do it is an unimaginative red herring designed to prevent the so-called redistribution of wealth most successful elite capitalists abhor. All that is really needed is creative problem solving. I believe the best way is to establish minimal taxes on new value created by robots and automation—the work tax or dividend capturing taxes. Funding UBI is not the problem; lack of imagination, moral outrage, and political will are.

Toward a Postcapitalist Plan for Trade and Distribution

Adam Smith's book *The Wealth of Nations,* published in 1776, is a seminal text in the history and development of capitalism, as well as a formative force in contemporary capitalist thought. It laid out many principles on trade, markets, price dynamics, and other foundations of capitalism, and those principles are still used to understand the system that dominates global economics today. If Smith's book lays out the basic principles of capitalism, we can turn to it to discover which aspects of the system will dissolve as the postcapitalist world emerges.

Central to Smith's idea was the theory of competitive advantage, which describes the basic rationale for trade. Each location has certain natural advantages over others—for example, climate, soil types, topography, and geographic location. Because of this, Smith argued that a city or nation should take advantage of its endowments by specializing in the production of goods amenable to that advantage, and then trade with others who are endowed with different advantages. The simple case? Minnesota should grow feed corn, and Florida should grow oranges. Sure, both states could try to be self-sufficient and grow everything themselves, but Minnesota orange trees would not survive winter, and Florida's soils would not grow feed corn well. According to Smith, Florida and Minnesota should grow what they are good at and trade with each other, thereby enhancing the wealth of each. Those who try to be self-sufficient and produce everything themselves are at a disadvantage.

Smith's idea works well enough in a capitalist world that operates according to his other theoretical concepts—the invisible hand of the market, the law of supply and demand, and the theory of economic actors operating from "enlightened self-interest." In the developing postcapitalist world, however, these theoretical concepts break down. Infinite supply of digital products destroys the law of supply and demand, markets fail, and people act in ways completely contrary to what enlightened self-interest is supposed to mean. Where does that leave the theory of competitive advantage? In this essay, we will examine that question as it befuddles some postcapitalist utopian thinkers and animates postcapitalist critics as well. I also want to discuss two related questions: What about distribution? and, if there are no markets, how will products be distributed around a globally interconnected economy?

The Elimination of Competitive Advantage

As we have seen, capitalism's own internal logic is going to lead to the breakdown of the market system by driving digitalization to cut costs, while the upshot will be the production of digital abundance. When digital supply is infinite and free, Adam Smith's law of supply and demand no longer functions, and the invisible hand of the market ceases to exist.

In addition, capitalism's push for globalization, together with technological innovation, is flattening the economic world and eliminating competitive advantage. This flattening is occurring in two ways. First, the supply chain outlined above is quickly becoming obsolete; it is not that shipping is automated, but that it will become unnecessary. There's a decreasing difference in advantages between one place and another—even in food production—because any digital product can be produced anywhere. Digits behave the same in Patagonia, Bangalore, or Phoenix, thus removing competitive advantages based on place. Economic geography becomes very flat indeed.

The second flattening of competitive advantage is happening in direct proportion to the rise of postcapitalism. In recent decades, the competitive advantages Adam Smith wrote about have changed in nature. When he wrote his book, competitive advantage was primarily derived from natural resources—for example, climate, minerals, power sources like rivers, and harvestable forests. Today, competitive advantage is defined primarily in terms of wage differentials, which are magnified by currency valuations. The differences in cost of labor caused the flight of capital from high-wage areas to low-wage areas, thus decimating the manufacturing base of many advanced industrialized countries.

As digitalization and automation are more widely adopted by businesses, the value of labor heads quickly to zero, and as it does so, wage and currency differentials become increasingly irrelevant. In mid-2016, Adidas announced it was moving production back to Germany from Southeast Asia.[35] Under traditional capitalism, this would be good news for Germany and the town where that factory was built because it would create jobs, locally patriated profits, and investment. The problem? Although the factory would produce 500,000 pairs of shoes per year, it would employ a mere 160 employees and not a single shoemaker.[36] In other words, the labor cost-driven competitive advantage of southeastern Asian countries is no longer an advantage—it has been undermined by the zero-labor cost of an automated factory. Under these conditions, the distance some Asian countries are from the market now represents substantial cost for shipping and distribution. When labor costs approach zero, production logically moves closer to the consumer market because such proximity also reduces cost to the manufacturer.

This upending of recent capitalist logic foreshadows a far more profound shift. We can expect automation, miniaturization, and digitalized abundance to bring factories closer to markets, but the trend will continue to close the distance between production and consumption. Under capitalism, we produced in the factory and consumed in the home. But as production gets smaller, digital, and more automated, production and consumption will come together under the same roof. As such, the structure of a separation of production and consumption also falls away as a meaningless relic of history. In its place, we expect a new postcapitalist order to emerge in which the co-location of production and consumption fundamentally changes the economic order.

Automated Distribution

Capitalism requires distribution because products are created at nodes of production, and once made, they need to be moved to nodes of consumption—for example, the corn needs to move from Minnesota to Florida, and oranges from Florida to Minnesota. Plus, nodes of production are capital-intensive, and whether the node is agricultural or industrial, they require land, buildings, and equipment. The need to move them gives rise to trucking, railroads, distribution centers, and stores.

One alternative is that the nodes of production remain as they are, and distribution becomes digitalized and fully automated. Here's the vision: You order the product online in a digital transaction automated by voice order, the product is picked from a warehouse by a robot, packaged by a robot, loaded onto a programmed, self-driving car that takes it to your home, and then the package is delivered to your doorstep by yet another robot. Such a disruptive approach to delivery service is certainly novel, but it would occur in the early stages of the transition to postcapitalism when capitalism is still hanging on. The capitalists will love it because of the drastically reduced distribution costs. While millions of people will be out of work, they will still need the products in those warehouses. Scarcity remains a dominant principle. Capital is intensive throughout the system—in the original production, in the warehouse, and in the robots and vehicles. Capitalists will replace labor throughout the distribution system, increase profit margins, and still protect their capital-intensive nodes of production.

On the receiving end of the system, this vision maintains consumers as consumers. We all buy what we need. It neglects that fact that income will be scarce because all the work is being done by robots or is automated. While consumer frustration could become impossible to contain and a popular revolt could erupt because of it, nothing in the architecture of the capitalist system has really changed. The vision is not postcapitalist at all—producers concentrate capital and produce, distributors concentrate capital to distribute, and consumers spend their capital in order to buy. The result? More capital for producers, less for consumers, and exacerbated inequality. In other words, automated distribution is a step in the process toward a truly postcapitalist scheme for the distribution of products, but is not, in and of itself, postcapitalist in nature.

Eliminated Distribution

As compelling as digitalized distribution may be, a truly postcapitalist economy will overturn the need for those distribution networks in the first place. In fact, it will eliminate the nodes of capitalist concentration within nodes of production, and instead develop a vision in which production and consumption are largely the same. In postcapitalism, the restrictions in national circumstances, which gave rise to Adam Smith's idea of competitive advantage, would be overcome by enabling production technologies located as near to the place of consumption as possible. In Adam Smith's world, producing oranges in Minnesota was ludicrous, but "digital oranges"—the kind that can be reproduced from a stem cell or, eventually, a genetic code— can be produced anywhere, and when they are, the theory of competitive advantage is rendered meaningless. Plus, through digital miniaturization, every household can produce everything it needs on its own, which means that large-scale trade and distribution are no longer needed.

This is not a prescription for drudgery or romantic peasantism. Instead, this postcapitalist vision will move the production of all goods that are digital and essentially free to produce to a level of individual production within the consumption unit—the home. Individuals will be far freer than they have ever been because they are no longer dependent on jobs, distribution systems, and automation. Instead, true economic freedom may be achieved—it will be supported by postcapitalist philosophy and enabled by new technologies.

Technology Distributed

Just which technology will play a significant part in this development? Three key capabilities will produce this merging of production and consumption—3D printing, digital food, and home-based solar energy.

3D printing will be as ubiquitous as laser printing is today. 3D printing will enable us to make most products ourselves once we acquire the architecture in the forms of digital 3D plans and designs. In the future, these plans will be free. Tools of the home such as plates, pots and pans, and cooking utensils will be the early items created, but it won't be long before more complex items can be printed from digital code—lamps, clothing, books, coffee makers, and eventually even computers and robots—or that parts are 3D printed and products are robotically assembled.

Likewise, it is possible that for very large items—say cars and picnic tables—a local infrastructure might make it possible to utilize industrial size 3D printers on an as needed basis. In a capitalist market world, such an idea would be anathema—considered socialist and just waiting for capitalist abuse. But in a world of digitalized abundance, there is nothing to gain from freely building more at no cost because no one would buy it anyway—there is no market. The vision is that a person needing a new picnic table goes to the 3D printing center with the appropriate digital code, plugs it in, and the picnic table is printed.

Second, digital food production, especially of meats, are developing rapidly. Several companies are doing this now based on stem cell technology. Their hope will be to disrupt and eliminate the food supply system that is based on animal production, and therefore change how we produce and obtain food.

Created as it is within the capitalist system, company leaders envision the establishment of production facilities and distribution of the products. But what if the technology to grow these food items could be miniaturized such that the production can be housed in a single-family home? Today, it appears easiest to produce ground meat products with this technology, but it is not hard to imagine that with genomic codes and proper digital guidance, one will soon be able to grow a T-bone steak with the same technology. If you can grow a steak without the cow, why can't you grow an orange without the tree? The point is that as this technology grows, it will eliminate the distance between production and consumption, and that will lead inevitably to a postcapitalist paradigm for trade and distribution.

Third, home-based production of energy, primarily through solar electric production, will relocate the source and system of energy production. Today, solar power is being driven by capitalist models, with huge "solar farms" covering acres and acres of land to capture the sun and convert it to electricity, which is then distributed over the grid. From a capitalist's viewpoint, this makes perfect sense, but it will never work in the postcapitalist era. It simply cannot be sustained in a postcapitalist world because there won't be the incomes to pay for and sustain it. It would be far cheaper for society to cover the roofs of houses and businesses with solar panels, thereby collecting all the energy needed right where it is needed. When done this way, distribution is irrelevant because production and consumption occur in the same place. Adam Smith's notion of competitive advantage is rendered meaningless.

Conclusion

Localized digital capability creates a truly level playing field that Adam Smith could not have imagined. The local advantages of soil and climate for food production, access to raw materials, access to power sources, access to labor markets, and even access to distribution nodes—they all evaporate in a digitalized postcapitalist era. What replaces them is access to the digital codes, knowledge, and capabilities to produce independently, and even those things will be produced digitally. Households will therefore produce and consume their own energy, produce and consume their own food, and produce and consume their own goods—all automatically using digital and robotic controls. As this radical transformation occurs, new economic ideas will necessarily emerge, and Adam Smith's ideas on the necessity and value of trade will be relegated to dust bins of history.

Capitalism, Postcapitalism, and Sustainable Economics

Capitalism and Sustainable Economics: Made for Each Other

For many decades, *sustainability* has been treated as an alternative economic approach to industrial agriculture, extractive mining, clear cutting forests, burning fossil fuels, and similar environmental horrors. Its leading ideas are to limit scale, trust the market if it offers a truly level playing field, avoid or eliminate government subsidies, and halt the impact of free trade. It promotes local production as much as possible, eating and consuming according to the season, and quality over quantity. I do not suggest that any of these ideas are bad ideas—it's just that they are not alternatives to capitalism.

Questions of scale, market, subsidies, and free trade are issues concerning the *substance* of capitalism. Sustainable farmers may have a different view of these issues, but they are still operating on and engaging the same basic economic principles. They invest capital in land, equipment, and livestock; they produce goods, which need to go to market; they are subject to market forces. Nothing in this framework of ideas is an alternative to capitalism itself—they are all capitalist ideas.

In fact, promoters of sustainability have gone to great lengths to prove financial viability for alternative enterprises *within* the capitalist system. Non-profits like the Land Stewardship Project and others organize and document case studies of the financial viability of various farms to encourage other farmers by showing them a path. They show not just the production methods, but also the marketing and financial methods required to sustain these enterprises in a capitalist system. For the most part, these studies are extremely useful. They open the door and show a new path. I used them, and many other independent farmers I know are using them as well.

The problem is that all these solutions of financial sustainability sit squarely within the capitalist system. This is understandable because capitalism was, and continues to be, the defining economic system within which sustainability must operate. Despite success in uncovering models that can work, this success is precisely why sustainability as a set of ideas will not be of much help in imagining the postcapitalist world. Sustainability, as it has been largely discussed and practiced, is not an alternative to capitalism—*it is dependent on it*.

Postcapitalism: A Challenge to Sustainable Economics Theory

Postcapitalism requires new thinking from sustainability theorists because the assumptions of sustainable economics no longer hold. A postcapitalist world driven by digitalization will not have functioning markets as their primary feature. It will be virtually impossible to price goods and services, including food. Labor will have no value, and eventually, capital won't either. What can sustainability even mean in such a world? How will sustainable economics work in a world where markets fail? Where labor has no intrinsic value? Where land and capital cannot be priced? The hallmark of sustainability is attempting to make alternative, sustainable enterprises work in a capitalist, market-driven world. If postcapitalism is not essentially a market-driven world, how can the principles of sustainable enterprises apply to a postcapitalist era?

Sustainable enterprises, which are inherently capitalist in nature, are essentially meaningless in a postcapitalist world. In postcapitalism, all businesses are sustainable because there is no existential threat to their success. Businesses are creative endeavors driven by passion rather than exploitative enterprises driven by greed or survival anxiety. Businesses may make the information sources for things like digital food production or 3D printing, but because there is no need, they really don't have to worry too much about sales. When sales and income no longer threaten businesses, every business is sustainable by definition.

My critique is not meant to damage sustainability. Today, we need more sustainability in farms, fisheries, forests, energy production, and consumer lifestyles. People understand instinctually that this is a better way to go in a capitalist world, even if they can't actually execute it in that same world! But as we look toward a postcapitalist future, it would be looking backward, not forward, to focus on sustainability. Postcapitalism is inherently sustainable because it undercuts the very nature of unsustainable practices. Extraction, hierarchy, and scarcity become curious anachronisms in a postcapitalist era, whereas the contemporary sustainability movement is one side of the dialectic argument focused against capitalist tendencies. How much better to render such ideas irrelevant, as postcapitalism does, than to fight on in an endless losing battle? Postcapitalism is, in fact, the only way to achieve true sustainability.

III

Postcapitalist Form and Governance

CAPITALISM IS COMMONLY UNDERSTOOD AS THE economic system of modernity, so it is easy to see the economic implications of capitalist collapse. Modernity, however, involves not just the particular economic system of capitalism, but also the procapitalist systems of politics (states and democracy) and religion (Christianity, in particular). What will the wider implications of a new postcapitalism be on these realms of human society? How comprehensive is this situation? These essays explore those implications, and set the stage for outlining a new postcapitalist society.

Postcapitalism, Networks, and the New Post-State World

Just as capitalism developed in a milieu of political, religious, and sociocultural norms, both affecting them and being changed by them, the postcapitalist era will do the same. Both in economics and in politics, everything will be different in a postcapitalist world. What will happen to the power of the state in a postcapitalist world? Why would the development of postcapitalism—an economic force—mean anything at all for the state—a political force? If postcapitalism does affect the state, what will that effect be? While we can't completely predict the outcome, we can define the forces at play to give a better sense of where it is all heading.

Capitalism and Its World

Capitalism emerged from a time in history when everything else was changing with it—church doctrines, social expectations, and governing structures all changed and reinforced each other over a similar time period. The rise of Luther's doctrine of unmediated experience of God moved the focus from priests as mediators to the individual's direct relationship with God. Followed by Calvin's outright embrace of capitalistic principles decades later, these changes turned previously unacceptable behavior, such as charging interest on loans and marking up goods for a profit, into religiously sanctioned activities. The new Protestant churches provided social structure to support these doctrines, and much later in the 18th century, even newer ideas such as secular humanism fought for preeminence in places like France, Germany, and England. The transition from the dominance of the church in virtually all matters of life in medieval times to a raucous contest of ideas and doctrines in subsequent centuries was part of what allowed capitalism to flourish. Hence, religion as we know it could only develop in a capitalist world, and capitalism could only develop in a religious environment allowing it room to breathe.

During the same period as capitalism's dance with religion, the political structures of the emerging modern world underwent enormous transformation. The pre-capitalist feudal period was characterized by local royal courts ruling over cities as independent states. In Italy, for example, city-states had separate rulers in Milan, Florence, and Venice, so much so that even a great artist like Leonardo da Vinci would relocate to see if he could find better patronage at a different court.[37] Each had its own currency and coinage, laws, customs, and dialects.

Capitalism, however, cannot flourish in an environment with this kind of structural diversity—it needs consistency to enhance trade and allow competitive advantages of location to benefit more people through trade. Capitalism needs consistency of currency and trade rules across a territory to preserve, deploy, enhance, and aggregate capital. It needs standards of weight, measurement, value, and transportation to create effective markets. While city-states preserved diversity, nation-states began to create consistent, level playing fields. Over time, capitalism and these larger scale states grew together because they needed each other and reinforced common goals.

The early states, however, still ruled through the power of nobility over subjects—a political vestige of the feudal period. Even early versions of democracy in places like England were more a congress of nobles than they were a power-to-the-people movement. Much later, in the 18th century and beyond, nobility gave way to the sovereignty of the people as a leading political idea, with enormous consequences for capitalism. The American and French Revolutions were explicit about this shift in political power, and in America the shift was reinforced economically as the government gave land—the country's capital—to individuals through the Homestead Act. Democracy energized capitalism as it had never been before, and capitalism enabled democracy by reinforcing the power of the individual citizen with economic reality.

While capitalism and democracy collaborated at the individual level, they also worked together at the structural level. Democracy won the buy-in of individual people to the notion of the state; self-government was a reasonable way to handle lawmaking and it gave legitimacy to the state. But the state and capitalism had far more in common than that. Both were built on similar principles—for example, rule of law, private property, and hierarchical control—so they reinforced each other as ideas and as a practical matter. The state grew its power and capitalism grew its wealth.

The Logic of the State vs. the Logic of Networks

One reason why capitalism and the state grew in power together is that they are based on the same logic. This can be seen by considering some key aspects of state logic.

- Like capitalism, the state is hierarchically structured. So-called representative democracy concentrates power toward the top within government. Its most extreme example of hierarchy is the military, in which a cult of reflexive duty dominates the military structure. Socially, hierarchy provides structural order, while for individuals it provides cover and the fundamental self-deceit that says, "It wasn't my decision." Corporations and government thrive on this idea.

- The state is coercive, but reciprocal. It can force people to do all kinds of things by denying them freedom. It can jail people. It can take their belongings. It can force military service. It always sets the laws. But at the same time, the people of the state are citizens, not subjects. People have stature and rights, which the state has a responsibility to protect. In many countries, the state is repressive and does not reciprocate, but as recent examples in Syria and Libya show, failed states are even worse.

- States protect and rely on extraction. They control land and access to land, and they enable the extraction of minerals, oil, lumber, food, and all other natural resources that feed the capitalist system. Because they allow this, standards of living generally increase, and this makes people happy, if also complacent.

- Closely related to extraction, states are profoundly geographically bound. They have definite borders, and states that cannot define their borders are usually either at war or barely functioning. When borders are violated, it is usually considered an act of war, a violation of sovereignty, or at least a profound offense. States are defined by their territory—a reality that capitalists require and exploit.

- States also unify systems and processes within their boundaries. They create official currencies, languages, laws, and procedures. To participate effectively and meet one's economic needs, one must comply. In this way, states create a level playing field so that capitalism can prosper—the more level it is, the more prosperous the system as a whole becomes.

- Finally, states are linear. They create rules and laws to have an effect. They are determinative, and sometimes systematic. But in all cases, they function linearly, like a process. One follows the bureaucratic steps one at a time to get things done—step by step by step. It is much like a capitalist assembly line; process driven, orderly, and linear.

These six points illustrate how state and capitalist logic are built on the same frameworks and principles. Postcapitalism will see the rise of governing structures that are very different and reflect the principles of the new *postcapitalist* world. So far, the only organizational structure to emerge after digitalization is the network. If we assume that networks become a dominant organizational structure of the postcapitalist era, what might that tell us about the new political structures to follow? As we will see, the principles of networks suggest that states will become less dominant as governing structures, if not outright irrelevant.

Here is how network-based principles might handle these same issues:

- Whereas states and corporate capitalism are primarily hierarchical, digital networks are inherently flat and egalitarian. They tend to be very wide and any voice or participant may contribute at any time. The only real barrier to participation is internet access, which is a real impediment for many people in the world. Nonetheless it is a much lower barrier to entry than, say, needing to get hired by a boss in a competitive interview process that puts the decision solely in the corporate or bureaucratic boss's hands. It is also a much lower barrier than having to get a meeting with a government official. And once one is in a digital network, that person is free to participate or not at their own discretion.
- Whereas the state is fundamentally coercive but reciprocal, the network is utterly voluntary. Networks have little power, mostly just influence. No one can command and control a network, and if they could, it won't be a matter of economic survival for the participant. Voices of greater or lesser influence will emerge within them, but influence is not power. They are communities of common interest, and as such, the most effective networks patrol themselves. This feature can be positive or negative—caring participants can protect a network and rally to a defense of its purpose, but they can also gang up in a version of digital vigilantism that virtually throws people out. The point isn't that the network is perfect, it's that it is different.
- Extraction is irrelevant to digital networks, and networks know no borders. They do not care inherently about geography. Most social and collaborative work networks span the entire globe, and national

borders are never even considered. Value is not obtained by extracting minerals; it is obtained by the value of the connection—its depth, importance, effectiveness, or quality. Contribution matters. So does engagement. And so does connection.

- Whereas states try to create level playing fields for capitalism through control of geography, networks only create level playing fields for communication, and geography is irrelevant. The one limitation is that networks need to communicate so they need to share a language, be it spoken, written, or even computer code. In today's world, language still has strong geographic components, but there is nothing inherent in the network requiring geography. As languages become ubiquitous, geography becomes irrelevant.

- State bureaucracies require and create conformity to the system, whereas networks enable individuals to contribute. Anyone can add their work, their ideas, their money, or their content to a network. The whole idea of a network is to enable this individual contribution. Within the network, access is largely flat and encouraged, partly because participation is a measure of value. States and capitalist structures tend to control through bureaucratic hierarchy, whereas networks tend to highlight based on interest.

- Finally, whereas states are linear and process driven, networks are exponential and driven by connection. In capitalist structures, cause leads to effect; in networks, passion leads to transmission. People advance things because they care, and the quality of the transmission, as well as the speed of the diffusion, depends primarily on how much they care. Exponential growth occurs so long as the care is present. When an idea or contribution goes beyond the place where people care, it stops being transmitted.

The difference between the two logics could hardly be more stark. If we are really transforming to a postcapitalist world in which networks will be the central organizing principle, it is reasonable to ask how the governing structures will change to accommodate the new world. It is clear that states are not set up to handle this new networked world; indeed, the very presence and development of networks, irrespective of their content or purpose, is essentially subversive to state-based forms of government (just as digitalization is subversive to capitalism). But what form of government will replace the state?

Possibilities for Replacing State Structure

The values of the networked world will drive the next form of government, and institutions that rise from within the networked world are likely to play a big role. No one knows what will actually happen, but we can speculate on a few possibilities:

- New global governing bodies will appear. While decisions may need to be made, rules created, and standards enforced, these bodies may also function much more like the digital communities they will govern. Influence will be far more important than power. Community participants who care enough may participate, add their voice, and even work for the organization, much like they do in collaborative communities like open source software production. Much of the check and balance is the community self-policing according to its own rules.

- Global communities, digitally connected by the internet, will outstrip the powers of the states of which we are currently citizens. Corporations will no longer be multinational, but rather, truly global. Entrepreneurs running one or three person businesses already often do business in multiple countries. Allegiance to a state or country will no longer matter, but connection to your community will because that is where most standards of conduct will actually be created.

- Direct democracy within the remaining countries is likely, and so is the use of direct democracy in global organizations. Direct democracy means that participants vote directly on the proposals that affect the community, rather than appointing representatives to do it for them. Within existing state structures, for example, it could be logistically practical for voters to participate on every issue, not just the occasional referendum. In many network communities, this is exactly how things operate. Perhaps more intriguingly, member participation is exactly how non-state postcapitalist institutions or networks will govern, and these non-state institutions will inevitably cross all formerly capitalist state boundaries.

The New Post-State World

Although many principles of the postcapitalist world are clearly emerging, we can only speculate on what will actually appear in terms of structures and organizations built upon those principles. The post-state world doesn't imply that states will no longer exist; it only suggests that their power and ability to govern will be severely restricted. On one side, these restrictions will be experienced as a decline in power and control, thereby giving rise to xenophobia in a world that seems to be falling part (and which, in fact, is falling apart!). This social problem is unavoidable because the structures that people rely on to organize themselves will be disempowered, and perhaps even disappearing altogether. As a social fact, many will experience this as disconcerting and confusing. On the other hand, as states lose power and are restricted, new forms of governance and enterprise are likely to emerge. These new forms present opportunity, excitement, and vitality to the governance process.

As this "post-state" world emerges, here are a few signs to watch for:

- Government structures will flatten so that less power is concentrated in elected officials, and more in the direct democracy of self-government. In the US, we will see this first as an increase in referendum governance, and later as direct democracy of, by, and for the people. Courts will emerge as the arbiter of conflicts between public opinion (majority rule) and individual rights (minority rights).
- States will be less important for day-to-day life than the international organizations administering the internet, the networks that guide our lives, and the rules of collaborative communities to which we belong, whether they are benign and social, critical and professional, or ideological and evil.
- The assertion of power through war, trade rules, and similar international instruments will dissipate, especially as an expression of the need for resources. As geography and the resources therein become less relevant, conflicts will center on ideology and have no clear territorial aims. The recent increase in terrorism may be the earliest incarnation of this reality.
- States will seek to maintain relevance as the bestower of benefits that are required to maintain capitalism, especially playing a role in social needs throughout the breakdown. We can expect this to include administering universal basic income programs, universal health care, and managing the finance system. Citizenship will be required to qualify for the benefits, thereby strengthening the state, albeit temporarily.
- The relationship between states and enterprises is likely to change. States will create more flexible structures to handle issues and disputes in the newly networked world—how to administer the

creative commons copyrights, manage global collaborations, and maintain networks. Over the long haul, as corporate capitalism loses its power, the state will become far less regulatory and also less relevant to the creative, economic work of individuals in the world.

Networks and collaborative structures will partially supplant and mostly change the state—that's what we mean by the post-state world. This is not necessarily a recipe for anarchy, but it will create stress, conflict, fear, creativity, opportunity, and heart-breaking loss. It is precisely this complication that makes the postcapitalist era what it is. It is no nirvana, nor will it be catastrophic. It will be different, and the more ready we are for that, the more we can embrace these changes which will inevitably come our way.

The Postcapitalist Meaning of Social Networks

At this early stage in the postcapitalist project, nothing is more emblematic of the new postcapitalist world than social networks. From a social standpoint, these networks operate on non-capitalist terms. Millions and millions of people are building and participating in networks without any fees or payment of any kind. Individuals develop friendships and communities of concern, and networked communities manage themselves as volunteer organizations with their own minimal structures but with flat hierarchies, levels of authority, responsibilities, and accountabilities. People participate as they do in other organizations they care about, all on a volunteer basis. They do this because of the value they receive in such participation, and they do not measure that value in terms of money.

Here are some of the things you can readily see people doing today:

- People use Facebook to enhance and drive their social life with family and friends.
- People build groups of common interest on Facebook, Meetup, online forums, Tumblr communities, and many other places.
- People build whole worlds of so-called fan fiction, design ideas, political sloganeering, and other "creative commons" types of work that offer free ideas, writing, entertainment, and so on—all work that in a capitalist world cannot be sold or monetized in the first place, and which also features zero marginal cost for reproduction because it is digital.
- People participate in collaborative, open-sourced projects like Linux, Tomnod, Wikipedia, and Sugar. They contribute their energy of their own free will—they are doing what they want to do.

New Focus of Connections

In many ways, these activities are obvious manifestations of the new digital network. More subtly, because of digital connections together with capitalism's ruthless treatment of employees, digitalization is changing worker affinities and allegiances. Identification with companies has been waning for decades, but the replacement was not clear until recently—people now identify more with their professional communities than they do with their employers, including for career advancement. In hundreds of interviews conducted as part of my consulting practice, a constant theme emerges— people express more allegiance and dedication to their professional or peer communities than to their employer. Plus, other than the annual conference when they actually see each other as people, their professional community relationships are almost entirely digital—email, listserves, LinkedIn groups, followers, and other digital manifestations.

This lateral connectivity with the profession reveals a fault line in capitalist hierarchy. The people that matter to one's career are decreasingly sitting at the top of the corporate hierarchy, and increasingly sitting in a similar office in another company. The digital revolution has made this possible as peer social networks are every bit as accessible as the corporate network. This development is more than the class solidarity of 19th century English workers whose affinity stayed with their class, while the power over their destiny laid with the capitalist bosses. This new development is putting the power for one's career in the network, not in the hierarchal structure. Few changes could be more subtle nor more decisive; they illustrate the early stages of a challenge to the capitalist hierarchy.

It is possible that worker allegiance to professional communities is the first postcapitalist social move, and it may presage a new social order. Under capitalism, social cohesion started in the family, and in recent decades it spread through the church and company. Then, at the highest level, it became allegiance to the country. Today, as social networking replaces the traditional routes for social cohesion, the social bonds at all three levels are coming apart, even within capitalism. Love of country is meaning less and less as social bonds spread across national boundaries through social networks. Corporate inversions illustrate the lack of allegiance to any country whatsoever, and entrepreneurial free agents collaborate as if national boundaries don't even exist. The same social networks connect us across companies so that career management has more to do with your digital conections than with your superiors at work. Many far flung families are finding social networking to be a great way to overcome the tyranny of distance, but others find the social network disruptive to in-person connection time, even at the family dinner table.

The point is that many of these networks, as they exist today, are digital, but the digitalization overlays a real connection with a real person. To that extent, it can be argued that these changes may not yet be postcapitalist in nature. The digital logic, after all, suggests that eventually, even in our so-called social networks, the people begin to disappear.

Fake Connections

Social networks are based on the underlying connections between people, but it turns out that in a digital world, people can be fooled into thinking they are connecting to people when in fact they are not. For example, have you ever screamed at a robocall? Have you ever gotten angry when an interactive voice response system didn't understand what you were saying?

Similarly, social networks are being run by automated services. Clever writers can trick you into thinking a person wrote something when in reality it is being served up automatically and on cue to develop interest and get you—a person—to "relate" to a brand image. Despite a certain abhorrence many people have for the deception, it is hardly even worth mentioning compared to what is coming. Machine learning and artificial intelligence will soon replace many people on these networks. Not only will the machine automatically post, but it will automatically *respond*. Indeed, AI will actually *converse*. Because the interaction is on screen or over an audio line, however, a person will have no way of knowing if they have a real person or a machine on the other end of the line.

If one thinks of such changes happening all at once, it is hard to escape the imagination of catastrophe. Fortunately, there is no need for that. The changes will be incremental, and as such, people will adapt. For those who don't realize when they are interacting with a machine, they will be victims, especially early in the transition. Those who get it will likely avoid such circumstances, and thereby we come full circle in the human name. Instead of placing authority in the fact of publication—in books, on TV, or on social media—we may weirdly come to trust the one thing we can't usually deny— our own experience. It may become such that the only thing one can really trust is the physical presence of another human being.

Attempts to Control and Monetize

In the early stages of the postcapitalist transition, capitalism will try to control networks, especially through monetization. Today, the attempt to monetize these networks occurs on several fronts. For example, once created, people make assumptions about the interests of the network, and then broadcast messages to the network as advertising. In essence, they are leveraging a 20th century model of mass communication, except that they believe the audience can be predicted to have more interest in what they offer than they did previously. In capitalism, this network is treated as a market, and its value is measured in terms of what it can get people to buy. But in postcapitalism, the prices of things people buy move toward zero, so the monetary value of this market is also likely to move toward zero over time.

A more interesting attempt to monetize these networks is subscription. Participants pay to participate, or they pay to participate at a certain level that they find useful and of monetary value. As a professional network primarily organized around the value of work, LinkedIn has been most successful in selling these premium subscriptions to users. LinkedIn and other sites that focus on professional networks are likely to see increased interest during the decline of capitalism as people look desperately for well-paid work in a world where the price and value of work is declining rapidly. It is fair to ask how much people will be willing to pay for access to jobs that either pay nothing or enable you to buy things that are otherwise free. Despite LinkedIn's current success, eventually, this model will collapse, too.

Finally, some people monetize their networks simply through contribution and financial support for their idea. Some are asking for the contribution directly on their own sites, while others use crowd funding sites on a project-by-project basis. Crowd funding is the most non-capitalist model of such monetization, for it promises no actual return on investment. In fact, it isn't even possible without digitalization, and this may be the one way to financially sustain networks during the transition period.

The Dystopic Avoidance of People

As postcapitalism develops, human beings are likely to become more comfortable interacting with digits than they are with people. Increasingly, we see this in young people today. For example, I have people from the millennial generation who work for me, and the hardest thing to get them to do is pick up a telephone and call someone. They simply won't do it. They will send an email or text and simply assume it is received on the other end. To the question, "Did you let John know he has to do x?" the answer comes back, "I sent him an email." The assumption seems to be that John is doing nothing but monitoring his email, and that those emails, once sent, are automatically received. The thing is that these millennials are probably right about their millennial peers—they *are* constantly monitoring the digits in their lives! As they maintain those habits and grow older, their assumption will be the dominant societal assumption, signifying the beginnings of a new postcapitalist social order.

This subtle preference for digital interaction over human interaction is in some ways understandable. Let's face it: people are difficult and messy. They can be emotional and unpredictable. They can also be mean and vicious. Beyond the avoidance of human interaction, we may expect to see the rise of social robots programmed to avoid all those messy emotions and mean spirited intentions. We may begin to call a robot our best friend because they are reliable, and then our social networks with robots on the other end will seem perfectly normal indeed.

A Postcapitalist Conclusion

Digital social networks provide tremendous advantages to users, but also risk social dystopias that could disrupt our core ideas of social normalcy. The networks imply both outcomes. We can also anticipate changes and effects that we cannot yet imagine. One thing we can know for certain is that social networks will not go away; they will be a part of the core infrastructure of our collective future. As such, they will change human experience and our perception of the world.

Currency, Inflation, and central banks in the digitalized economy

What happens to the institutions of cash when cash no longer matters? That's the question society will face in the next 100 years as capitalism wanes into a distant memory, and the digitalized economy rises. If this thesis is correct, one must explore the implications, and at first blush that the consequences are nowhere so profound as those on the international monetary system, its central banks, and the national currencies—in the form of savings, investment, and debt—hungover from the capitalist era.

Here is a quick review of the postcapitalist thesis: a largely digitalized economy in which goods and services are digital means an unlimited supply of those goods at near zero prices. When supply is infinite at no marginal cost, markets can no longer effectively price goods according to supply and demand. Just as capital replaced craftsmanship and aristocracy, digitalism is going to replace capital and markets. And the prices of everything will tend toward zero.

As I write in early 2016, we are already in an era of historically low interest rates, which effectively prices the time value of money at zero. During this period, the great worry of most central bankers has been the prospect of uncontrolled deflation—a world in which prices are spiraling downward and therefore economic activity crawls to a standstill. Although leading economic institutions have successfully held off that prospect so far, the movement of rates toward zero creates unpredictable activity. Nonetheless, we have been in it so far for about seven years, and we have learned a few things about how these players will behave.

To begin with, operating corporations have absolutely hoarded cash. The reasons are simple: fear and lack of return. The 2008 debt crisis scared many corporate leaders, and a normal reaction is for those leaders to accumulate cash to head off the next shock. Predictably, they tend to do this when the memory of the problem is recent, and as time goes on, they will forget those fears and eventually loosen up the spending to invest for the growth and future of their business. But so far, that has not happened. Instead, corporate cash coffers have swelled. Investment opportunities are hard to find. The cash has been partly used for acquisition activity, but much of it is being deployed in dividends and stock buybacks, which are increasing apparent returns even while actual business activity is relatively stagnant overall.

What's interesting about this is the logic behind it: companies have made large amounts of money, but they are not finding effective ways to invest it—neither in real business operations nor in holding or loaning cash for a return. Bonds don't work because interest rates are near zero, and investment in operations doesn't work because there aren't many new markets or productivity technologies that can make a sizable difference at this time. While cash remains the lifeblood of any business in a capitalist economy, it is turning out that excess cash is increasingly useless. As a result, corporations are returning cash to stockholders in the form of record dividends and stock buybacks.

It is certainly premature to declare cash as utterly irrelevant, but this glimpse into the non-use of cash for investment and business may provide a window into that world in which cash will eventually be meaningless. With the great accumulation of corporate cash, corporations are basically saying that they can find nothing better to buy or invest in that will make their businesses more productive. For individual businesses, this is often the part of the business cycle known as "harvest" in which a company doesn't invest anymore. Usually, its technology or business model has become so outdated that it is cheaper to simply pull what one can from the business and, if anything, start something completely new rather than try to remake itself. Today, it appears that a huge chunk of the corporate sector is in the harvest stage.

But extracting cash through harvest is far different from deploying it effectively. On one hand, these buybacks and dividend payments are rational acts for these leaders to take, and they are bound to take them in shareholder interests. On the other hand, it shows the conundrum of a society where nothing is worth buying.

Consider, for example, the situation in which some people are earning cash from the value of their labor, but what is needed for ordinary life is exceedingly cheap and in abundant supply. Food is digitized, energy is cheap and comes from the sun, information is free. People accumulate cash but there is nothing to do with it. Loans return a zero interest rate—or maybe even negative interest— and there is little or nothing to buy, and what you would buy is cheap and requires little cash. One may use cash to start a company, but the products will be information-rich and prices will tend toward zero, so why not just do what inspires you—the money doesn't even matter anymore. Work is getting you cash but there is nothing to do with the cash, which leaves one wondering, why work?

This question—why work?—is directly analogous to the question corporations appear to be asking today—why invest? Most likely, this attitude of corporations is temporary and there will be additional cycles of investment in the coming century, but the digitalized economy creates a very similar logic. As excess cash cannot be deployed effectively, it will become increasingly worthless. There's no value to holding it, no value to spending it, and no value to earning it. Prices will tend toward zero based on the elimination of the marginal cost of production. This lack of spending is directly analogous to deflation as it appears in a normal capitalist economy. Deflation is signaled by price declines, but the real issue is a lack of economic activity *as capitalism measures it.* Deflation occurs when economic activity slows because consumers are acting rationally in response to economic and current conditions. In other words, deflation is the classic reason to stop spending, but cash worthlessness in an abundant economy is another.

As cash becomes irrelevant to consumers, prices collapse, and consumption fails to drive the economy, central bankers will be prone to colossal mistakes. They will likely view these changes through the eyes of historical capitalism, and not realize the changing nature of the economy. It is easy to imagine the adoption of policies to fight deflation with conventional methods—cheap money, lower interest rates to stimulate borrowing, and even the newer strategy of quantitative easing. But these strategies will simply reinforce the core problem, not fix it. Policy makers may even try going the opposite direction—increasing interest rates to increase returns on debt, for example. Neither approach will work, however, because it isn't money supply that is causing the economic discontinuity—it is digitalization pushing prices down by creating infinite supply of product. Corporate coffers are full of cash today largely because of quantitative easing and zero interest rates. Excess cash adds to the perception that cash is less relevant, and it creates a situation in which a business leader can't do anything with the money but return it to stockholders. More monetary policies oriented in the same direction will only add to that problem.

In fact, we seem to be seeing this today. Historically low interest rates and massive quantitative easing in the Unites States have not created an inflationary spiral at all. The accumulation of cash in corporate accounts seems to have triggered a bull market in stocks, but the labor market has not seen an increase in wages. Part of this, no doubt, is the increase in global competition for work, but part of it may also be the early indications that the late 20th century formulas which balanced inflation through money supply and interest rates is no longer working. Zero interest rates and abundant cash are supposed to stimulate investment by business and consumption by consumers, and trillions of dollars in cash should lead to inflation, but neither has happened.

The question is, why not? One possibility is that the downward pressure on certain prices is decreasing the overall circulation of cash. Today, that downward pressure is visible only at the edges of the economy, but those edges are usually capitalism's growth engines. Edges are where innovation happens, new markets are opened, and the major profits created. Today's edges are digital, however, and as a result, they cannot sustain their prices.

This is why central bankers are in trouble. Downward pressure on prices caused by digitalization can't be changed by monetary policy. Rather, declining prices is a result of digital abundance. Even if central banks cut rates, increase the money supply, and quantitatively ease, today's digital trends persist. If the central bankers go the opposite direction and increase interest rates, there may be more incentive to invest in debt to get a return, but it doesn't fix the problem of why you need more cash in the first place. Business leaders won't borrow because cash is not what they need.[vi] Prices are still likely to be falling in an environment of abundance and zero marginal cost of production.

For the most part, the central bankers will work to maintain the status quo, some with moderation and others with increasing alarm. They will look at data, try to assess the economy, determine ways to pull it out of recession, slowdowns, secular stagflation, or whatever other terms they develop for the

---

[vi] According to multiple news reports, Gary Cohen, the economic adviser to President Trump at the time spoke to a large number of CEOs and asked them to raise their hands if they would expand investment with cash savings from significant tax cuts. Only a few hands went up, and Cohen was left wondering why. The reason is corporate leaders don't need more cash, they need profitable investment opportunities. Digitalization is eroding prices, and therefore undercutting most investment opportunities they might otherwise seek.

coming malaise. They will adopt inconsistent and contradictory policies between countries, and lurch from one approach to another within countries. Their efforts are likely to fail because they can't see the basic fact that the capitalist system the banks underpin is waning. Our current period is not like the 1930s, nor the 1950s, nor the 1980s. We are simply in our own unique time in history when the dominant economic model is transitioning from capitalism to a postcapitalist era. New rules apply, and the bankers do not and will not understand those new rules while the bastions of capitalistic wealth and stability of the system feel threatened. When those influences arise, the bankers will undertake their most desperate and dire actions. Their ability or inability to resist those demands and that temptation will determine the level of suffering that occurs through this transition.

What Will Corporations Do in a Post-Capitalist World?

American corporations are formed to aggregate, create, manage and distribute capital—that's why they have become the dominant institution of American capitalist life. Their structural privileges, like limited liability and lack of mortality, further that single purpose of increasing capital. If that is true in a capitalist society, it begs a question: What will happen to corporations in a post-capitalist society? The answer is simple and brief: corporations as we know them will wane and eventually disappear.

In their place, the network will be preeminent, though some have argued otherwise. One group argues for capitalism's 250-year antagonist—the socialist state, albeit in new form.[38] Others argue for a new "caring economy," and still others for outright communism. But none of these are *structures*—they are simply value systems imposed on top of capitalism. Networks, on the other hand, are structural, and more importantly, they are alternative. Networks don't assume capitalism exists, and they provide a different way of organizing society.

How Are Networks Different than Corporations?

Plenty of business books have been written about the power of networks and collaboration, and corporations are trying very hard to put networks at their disposal. Corporate leaders want to enhance networks and increase collaboration, but only to a point. They still want to control the information. Networks operate very differently from the rules, standards, procedures, and hierarchy of corporate organizations. What do I mean? Consider these inherent aspects of how networks operate.

Network Participation is Free

First, participation in most networks is free. Capitalists are trying desperately to close networks and charge for access, but the most important networks, vis-à-vis the capitalist economy, are free, and many more are coming.

Today's young people expect networks and information to be free, and they are bringing that expectation to the organizations they work with. They are spontaneously building free networks and online communities in virtually all areas of life—social concerns, professional interests, business concerns, sports interests, health and wellness, and so on. While capitalists keep trying to build "premium membership areas" they can charge for, there seems to always be a person or organization willing to push the free line even further, and this is undermining and revolutionizing dozens, or even hundreds, of business models. Craigslist, which is mostly free, pretty much single-handedly destroyed classified advertising for the newspaper industry. Wikipedia destroyed World Book Encyclopedia and Encyclopedia Britannica, as well as Microsoft's early encyclopedia on CD-ROM. Similar forces are emerging in financial advice, marketing, sales training, and virtually every other human interest area.

Networks Are Content Agnostic

Second, networks are content agnostic, while also being content centered. They do not deploy capital. While corporations measure value by their effectiveness at deploying capital, as a structure, networks are concerned with connection, participation, engagement, and collaboration. Networks are driven by the passion and interest of the people in them. Content drives interest and engagement because that content is what people are passionate about. The actual content can be anything—the network structure does not care.

Two additional points should be made about the network's focus on content. First, it is the exact opposite of the mechanism corporations use to focus their people. Inherently, corporations abstract everything into money such that the content of a dispute or thing is not relevant—only its monetary value is relevant. People are coerced to participate in corporations because of the need for money or the need for what the corporation sells. In the network, content, including social content and ideas, is the only reason to participate, and it is never reduced to mere dollars. No one is coerced at all; participation is voluntary. People participate because of their passion, commitment, and engagement, not money.

The second additional point is that the content can be almost anything. Networks can emerge to create Wikipedia, but they can also emerge to create ISIS or even to serve a corporate purpose. The ideas they promulgate matter, and often take on their own force in the world. The differences in content between netowrks is irrelevant to their impact on a new postcapitalist world because it is the form and the structure that is different. This bias of networks is distinctly different from that of corporations. In corporations, *function* drives *money*, whereas in networks, *ideas* drive *connection*.

Networks as a Mode of Production

The final way that networks differentiate themselves is this—*networks are actually a mode of production*. They enable collaboration projects ranging from open source software to art collaboratives, Wikipedia-style projects, communities of interest, Uber-style gig employment, and crowd-sourced funding. They replace—or at least reorganize—the employment relationships, and they completely deflate the arguments of risk and reward used to justify—often rightly so—what adds up to the exploitation of workers by capitalists. The claim is that the huge investment in capital must generate a return on investment, and therefore capitalists can charge a premium for work that others have done. When people can choose to participate in a production network with only a computer or phone costing less than $500, capital has ceased to be the issue. In this sense, networks are dramatically changing how we will produce goods and services in the postcapitalist world.

Network Bias

If the thesis is correct that networks will organize the postcapitalist world, we may postulate that just as the values inherent in the corporate structure permeated our world in the past, those inherent in network structures will do the same in the future. Because those values are dramatically different, we can expect a very different impact on the world. To make a guess, let's consider how capitalism infiltrated society with its values so we can understand how the same will happen with networks.

The Corporation and Its Impacts

The corporation is the most unique and powerful institution of capitalism. Small, medium, or large, corporations are the mechanism by which capital operates. They enable society to organize the aggregation of capital and investment. They accumulate capital throughout their lifetimes. They invest, reinvest, and distribute capital as desired according to the narrow, capital accumulation and return on investment (ROI) interests of shareholders. Indeed, the corporation is designed specifically to gather, accumulate, deploy, and invest capital at a profit. As a structure, it does so magnificently well.

The central reason for corporate efficiency in investment and profit-making is a unique set of legal obligations undertaken by its board, officers, and employees. People in these roles are obligated to maximize value to shareholders through their function, and that nearly always means growing sales and profits. That obligation has real impact—whether people agree with it or not, the fact of their employment requires them to put their best efforts toward the "success of the business". Failure to do so will result in discipline or dismissal at a minimum, and can even land people in prison for shirking their fiduciary duty.

The corporate structure successfully forces individuals in corporate employment to put their own personal concerns or objections to corporate behavior on hold, and harnesses their energy, attention, and work to meet the corporate goal—irrespective of what it might mean for anything else in the world. One excellent example of this separation involved the 1986 Union Carbide disaster in Bhopal, India. Jerry Mander describes it this way:

> *"In 1986, Union Carbide Corporation's chemical plant in Bhopal India, accidentally released methyl isocynate into the air, injuring some 200,000 people and killing more than 2,000. Soon after the accident the chairman of the board of Union Carbide, Warren M. Anderson, was so upset at what happened that he informed the media that he would spend the rest of his life attempting to correct the problems his company had caused and to make amends. Only one year later, however, Mr. Anderson was quoted in Business Week as saying that he had 'overreacted,' and was now prepared to lead the company in its legal fight against paying damages and reparations. What happened?"* [39]

Mr. Anderson first reacted to the disaster as any human being would; then his role as head of Union Carbide required him to act according to a different set of principles. As head of the corporation he recognized no other responsibility but the company's profitability. It might be possible to criticize Mr. Anderson for his moral failing as a human being, but that is beside the point; had he stayed with his original reaction, he certainly would have been replaced as the head of the corporation by someone more amenable to the corporate goal. Hence, the corporate drive continues irrespective of the individual's choice.

The ability to focus millions of people's best energies on such very narrow goals has been the primary engine behind capitalist economic growth, especially since the Industrial Revolution. But it has also had consequences.

The prevalence of the corporate structure and way of thinking has turned virtually every aspect of society into a monetary, capitalistic transaction—and it is not limited to business. For example, freeways and airports require the government to acquire land that is already occupied. When the government decides to acquire a certain place, the tragedy of the destroyed neighborhood is "compensated" with the dollar value of the homes—and nothing for the relationships lost, the history lost, the friendships destroyed. Similarly, when corporations do wrong, the penalty is transformed into the only language the entity understands—money. People die from lung cancer and tobacco companies pay money by way of lawsuits for the damages, as if that were adequate compensation for a life. Even social concerns translate into money. The Roman Catholic Church covers up the sexual abuse of boys, and the boys must sue the Church to get the only kind of restitution the Church knows—money. Parts of the Church were bankrupted, but it still continues. For almost everything, the only remedy is money. This is why capitalism seems "normal" to us—its perspective has infiltrated everything.

The internal logic of the corporation drives it inevitably toward certain business outcomes and practices. The problem isn't that the company is bad, it is that the structure of organization predetermines its style, and therefore the general direction of its outcomes. Corporate organization forms these outcomes in nearly all activities, but alternatives are now available.

How Networks Are Different

Networks provide a different intrinsic value set that could similarly infiltrate society and shape how we all view the world. While corporate values gave rise to and reflect time-honored ideas like rule of law, private property, time value of money, duty, and obedience because capitalism required it, networks carry intrinsic values such as choice, ideas, volunteerism, interest, parallelism, egalitarianism, and fascination. These values are intrinsic to networks, and are needed for them to operate. Whether the content is utopian and idealistic, practical and productive, or hateful and virulent, the network itself still operates on the basis of these network values. This reality is why the rise of networks will eventually alter the cultural landscape.

What about the enterprise?

Since we are asking the question, "What will corporations do?" let us answer it directly—they will disappear. Corporations became the dominant capitalist structure because they were so good at protecting and gathering a return on capital. Postcapitalism won't be mature until digitalism destroys most markets, thereby eliminating the possibility of return on capital. In that kind of world, there is no reason to protect capital because the entrepreneur can't do anything meaningful with it anyway. As a result, there is no need for corporations, so they will vanish. In their place, new kinds of enterprises will arise, and they will be dependent on the network form of organization, not the corporate form. The eventual outline of these enterprises is impossible to fully predict, but we can see four vectors already emerging in the new digital economy.

First, as production goes digital, it will also become intensely local, and by "intensely local," I mean that production and consumption will intersect, probably at the level of the home. This is not about supporting a nice local shop you support down the street—that can happen within capitalism. Rather, digitalization will mean that production and consumption units come together, thereby ending their capitalist separation. For example, food, books, 3D printed goods, and abundant energy will all be produced at the level of the individual household or business. The valuable part of all products will be the digital plans for production, and those will be traded at no cost over internet-base networks. Plug the plan into the 3D printer, and you get the products you need.

Second, stores and shops will become less relevant, as will traditional capitalist distribution systems. Anything not produced in the home will be ordered online—thereby eliminating the need for stores—and robots and drones will get it to your door—utterly disrupting the existing distribution infrastructure. These changes will appear very soon, but as production becomes increasingly local, as described above, even this new system will give way to home based production.

Third, collaborative networks will be the source of most inventive and innovative activity, and the products will be viewed as property of the commons. "Enterprise" will mostly be carried out in these networks. Through them, people will develop interesting digital products and ideas, then disseminate them to the world. The network becomes both producer and disseminator, as well as consumer and user. Participation is driven by interest, and collaboration by the need to scale.

Conclusion

As capitalism declines over the next hundred years, the corporate structure will decline with it. Certainly, some corporate organizations will endure, but they will no longer define our cultural and economic reality the way they do today. Instead, networks will gradually take their place as the predominant way of organizing enterprise. New skills and capabilities will be needed to thrive and contribute, and new ways of producing will infiltrate nearly all of our production and provision of services. We won't work for companies; we will contribute to projects. In so doing, we will create a very different world than any one has experienced before.

What Do B Corporations Mean?

Capitalism is sowing the seeds of its own destruction. From stock markets to eBay to Amazon.com, digitalization of markets is already occurring. The digital component in relevant products has driven down prices to levels at which proprietors operating stores selling those same goods can no longer compete. Digital networks are rising to render state power obsolete, and to create digitalized goods that were previously impossible. In this milieu, structural changes are beginning to take hold as well. The Public Benefit Corporation, or B Corporation, is a new form of incorporation which signals that the traditional C and S Corporations are no longer meeting the needs of society.

Over the past decade, many states have changed their statues to allow the B Corporation form of organization. Whereas the traditional C Corporation must be managed to maximize profit and shareholder value, a B Corporation may manage itself to a double bottom line. In other words, shareholder value is one piece, and community or public benefit is another. On one hand, this creates new responsibilities for leadership; on the other, it relieves leadership of the sole fiduciary responsibility traditional corporate structures enforce. B Corporations declare that they are founded to not only create a return for shareholders, but also to deliver some public good. In some cases, the nature of that public good must be identified in the organization's articles of incorporation, while in others it may be a general public good to be defined and managed by the board and leadership.

The traditional corporation has one purpose and one purpose only—to manage and accumulate capital on behalf of its shareholders. Some inspired leaders found ways to add a social or public purpose to the mission of the company, but that mission had to be understood as adding to the gains of shareholders. Indeed, leadership has a legal, fiduciary obligation to make sure that what they do adds to that wealth for shareholders. If it did not, they would be violating this responsibility, and could be fired, sued, or, in an extreme case, imprisoned.

A traditional alternative is the non-profit corporation, which is generally tax exempt and funded by individual or corporate members, donors of one kind or another, or by grants from foundations or government. Non-profits have no profit-making requirement whatsoever, and in fact, many non-profit CFOs focus on balancing the books to show no profit every year. Although they may run small business as part of their operations, most non-profit corporations don't rely on those operations for funding.

This state of affairs, in which the two primary choices are for-profit corporations and non-profit corporations, made it impossible for businesses with a social conscience to contribute to the social or public good in a meaningful way. In fact, C-corporation leaders who tried were usually sued or removed by the board for violating their fiduciary duty. Non-profits, on the other hand, could try to do social good, but were dependent on the donors—most of whom earned their money through the system—often corrupting the non-profit on one hand, or limiting its effectiveness by depriving it of funds. Thus, people who wanted to start businesses and contribute to the social good were always in a conflict of interest, and therefore, the best energy and the best minds could not be brought to bear on our biggest social, environment, and public problems.

As an innovative new structure, the B Corporation enables corporate leaders to avoid this conflict. It frees them to be able to utilize and deploy corporate resources according to the mission of the B Corporation charter, even if it is not necessarily serving the accumulation of wealth for shareholders. Where authorized, the B Corporation is optional, but it represents a dramatically different set of possibilities in economic organization. Much of capitalism's incredible power over the last two and a half centuries has derived from the corporate structure and its intrinsic requirement for a single-minded focus on return to investors. States that chartered C and S corporations provided a unique privilege to these institutions to have such single-minded focus, and in return, the state benefitted from growth, economic development, and jobs. Companies were able, and even required, to focus exclusively on profit, wealth, and capital. This focus ran all the way up and down the line. It aligned boards, executives, and employees at every level, and made it so that the only way to justify activity was by meeting one of the four universal business needs—increase sales, decrease costs, improve productivity, or compliance with the law. Until the B Corporation came along, those were the *only* four legitimate things for the corporation and its employees to focus on.

In the big picture, this new B Corporation represents another crack in the capitalist armor. It is an admission by society that the limited focus of C and S Corporations are restricting what people sense as good and possible. It shows that people want to focus on more than just money, wealth, and shareholder capital. It exposes a desire by people to take resources that corporations can accumulate and use them for better purposes. Finally, it shows that human beings are more than the so-called "economic man;" we have a wholeness that goes beyond those classical definitions, beyond utilitarian self-interest, and beyond rationality.

Further changes in the system are likely to occur as this corporate form is adopted more widely, and the rules around its governance are developed. It should be pointed out, however, that while this form has been championed by many progressive critics of the capitalist system,[40] the statutes do not define "public good," and it is not a stretch to imagine that people not working for the public good will utilize the same structure—much as the non-profit structure has been adopted by industry groups who clearly do not have the public good in mind. B Corporations could just as easily be led by boards that are ideologically or religiously driven, for example, and whose sense of "public good" doesn't really comport with what one might expect that term to mean. Many industry associations, for example, are non-profit corporations, and are supported by enormous donations to carry out the public policy desires of the members. In the current state of B Corporation development, there is nothing to stop these structures from being used in the same way.

Nonetheless, the phenomenon of the B Corporation is worth examining precisely because it derives from a growing sense among cultural critics and activists that the structure is the problem. People are beginning to understand that the corporate structure is no longer serving the public good, but rather it is stealing the public good. It is the source of the damage, and it needs to be changed. The B Corporation is an attempt to change the structure within the context of the capitalist system, and it is worthy attempt. The growing awareness of critics and activists means we will be prepared for the next opportunity, and that is important indeed.

I see the B Corporation as a harbinger of the postcapitalist era. It holds a mirror up to the straight-jacket society has been placed in by the corporate structure as we have known it, and it reflects an effort to do something about it. The B Corproation indicates that as digitalization, which we mentioned in the opening, spreads and disrupts the capitalist system, more and more people are prepared to look for and consider alternatives. The B Corporation could play a role in providing those alternatives early in the transition to postcapitalist society, but in the end, even they will give way to other structures more amenable to new the postcapitalist world.

Does Postcapitalism Mean Post-Democracy?

While it seems to me that a postcapitalist era is an eventuality driven by the intrinsic logic of capitalism itself, the way it actually unfolds remains unknown. That's because while the logic leads to the inevitability of digital abundance, the breakdown of markets, the inability to expand into new markets, and the end of externalities, there is nothing to guarantee how human society responds. That people will respond is for certain, but how—what forms and political structures we will eventually adopt, what economic and social architecture we will create, the impact they will have on society and the global ecological and economic systems (as well as the people in all corners of the earth)—these things we cannot know because they all lie in the future.

Now that Paul Mason has really put the term *postcapitalism* on the intellectual and political map, the traditional right and left are responding energetically. The left, which needs a compelling new vision to replace the failure of communism and the ongoing failure of protest politics, has grabbed onto the idea of postcapitalism, and bent it to its own purposes—i.e., toward socialism and an idealism of the future. Conservatives, on the other hand, will see the vision of a post-work world as immoral. They will seek to defend the "sanctity of work," for example, as a blessing from God and something hallowed for believers to engage, even though the real purpose for celebrating the sanctity of work is to bless the exploitation of labor, which is the centerpiece of capitalist social arrangements.

From my own standpoint, they all have it wrong because they are arguing the issue from a capitalist ideological position, and the argument is limited to the economic realm. If there really is an inevitability to the postcapitalist era, it won't affect *only* the economic system, the 1 percent or the 99 percent, or the way we distribute goods and services. If and when postcapitalism occurs, it will change *everything*, we must consider the remainder of western ideology that is tied to capitalism, for it will surely change.

For example, capitalism is a handmaiden with democracy. The two rose together in historical and ideational synchronicity. The original inklings of western democracy, the magna carta, arose in an effort by English barons to protect their land capital and rights to profits from an acquisitive king. Private property and rule of law—two of the greatest principles underlying democracy and capitalism—arose well before our American Revolution, and continue to underpin our society to this day. That revolution for democracy was also a defense of capital, and it was fought at the very same time Adam Smith was writing and publishing his classic work, *The Wealth of Nations*.

If democracy and capitalism are thus tied together, then it is not a big leap to assert that when capitalism goes, democracy will also come under presuure. It would be wise to ask: What is postdemocratic? What is post right-left politics? Or, what is post the status quo political system? Let's explore.

Speculations on Postcapitalist Politics

Here are some thoughts on what a postcapitalist political system might look like. These are highly speculative and meant to provoke discussion, not to lay down a definitive idea, and I always welcome feedback and ideas on these thoughts.[vii]

- **Post-election:** In democracy, the power of the vote every year is the primary citizen franchise. We are all too busy working, raising families, trying to live the American dream or some other promise of getting ahead. People take their vote rather seriously. But in a postcapitalist politics, one possibility is that because people work less, they are more involved in self-government. Representatives become obsolete. Instead, people may vote far more regularly. As voting becomes electronic and digital, there is little reason why every issue can't be put to the people. The people vote directly on legislation, not for representatives who are beholden to special interests and who earn votes by either being the least bad option or by winning blind party loyalty. Representative democracy could become obsolete, and self-government might become an actual reality as digitalization diffuses into our political processes.
- **Post-mandate:** A post-capitalist politics would likely be liberated from any claim of mandate. If there are elections, elected officials would take a real approach to representing the complications of their constituency, rather than claiming a mandate from victory to vote the way they want to. This, in and of itself, would be a dramatic change.

[vii] Please write to me at postcapfuture@signorelli.biz if you have something to add.

- **Post-party politics:** Postcapitalist politics would be post-party politics. What I mean by this is that the hegemony the parties enjoy in the houses of Congress might be eliminated. We might move from a "majority rules" to a "plurality influences" kind of politics. There are many mechanisms for this, including the rights of the houses of Congress to create their own rules. That right puts all the power with parties, and if we maintain houses of Congress, it may be far more liberating to the human spirit to let people vote their representative conscience instead of voting their party affiliation. The way Congress is structured today, that will not happen. A postcapitalist politics, however, creates that opportunity.

- **Post-protest:** In the postcapitalist era, the politics of protest will dissipate as an obsolete anachronism. People will be heard and enfranchised directly into the system, rather than sidelined through power plays and asserted mandates. If people are enfranchised via direct voting on key issues, marches become displays and recruitment vehicles, but they aren't exactly protests that "speak truth to power" anymore. The power is with the people already. The hard lines that drive these protests will disappear because the fear of a "slippery slope," which drives most hard lines, will no longer hold sway, and cooler minds will prevail. Protest politics is based on fear and scarcity—two key aspects of the capitalist worldview. A right-left approach to these new politics will continue the polarization and eventual collapse. When scarcity and fear leave the equation, ideological positions may dissipate, and that may usher in an all new political era that affects not just the big picture, but also the local and even individual picture. I submit this: we will think differently about our politics in a world of abundance than in a world of scarcity, and that will affect our political calculations and perceptions, as well as the laws and regulations we think are needed.

- **Post-scarcity:** In a world of scarcity, politics is about the allocation of the scarce resources available. It tells who gets what, where the power lies, and what will be taken from whom to give to someone else for some ostensibly noble or public purpose. How could it be anything else? In corporate capitalism, it is largely about ameliorating the effects of the corporate privilege of focus on profit and unfettered capital aggregation and accumulation. A cynic might say it is about appeasing the people to allow the corporate to continue. In any case, the postcapitalist world of abundance gives the lie to all these impulses, no matter what side you are on. Politics is no longer about who gets what, because everyone has plenty. Politics is really about defending abundance against the human drive for greed, which will rise and fall no matter how much abundance we actually have. But this is a very different politics! It will seek to unleash creativity without the need to protect capital. It will reform the logic of our institutions—corporations, academia, religion—so that they contribute to the abundance, rather than protect their own little corner of scarcity. And, it will eschew power emanating from these institutions, preferring instead the power of the people enjoying their abundance. At least, these are possibilities that could fixate our new postcapitalist politics, and if they did, it would create a very different political climate.

The postcapitalist era represents a profound change in the standard order. Just as capitalism came into being and developed along with democracy and new religious doctrines promulgated through the Reformation, postcapitalism will only flourish when the appropriate state and religious frameworks join it. Political and religious frameworks will need to reflect, embrace, amplify and feed off of similar structures—for example, networks, collaborative communities, and digital representation. In other words, we are talking not just of a postcapitalist economy, but of a postcapitalist *world*. *Everything* will be postcapitalist, and that's when we will know that the change has really arrived.

IV

Two Crucial Books

I NEVER PASSIVELY READ A BOOK. RATHER, I READ TO argue. I take notes. I mark things up. To me, reading is an action-oriented, intellectual activity, and the mark of a good book is one that that is provocative enough to stimulate a good argument. The two books in this section, one by Paul Mason and the other by Nick Srnicek and Alex Williams, did exactly that. These books opened my eyes to the possibilities of postcapitalism. Each book has its strengths, and each has its shortcomings. But the two together lay the foundation for thinking about the postcapitalist future. Plus, I really enjoyed the argument.

Arguments with Postcapitalism: A Guide to Our Future, by Paul Mason

Capitalism is inevitably going to collapse over time. The reason, which is a central theme of Paul Mason's book *Postcapitalism: A Guide to Our Future*, is a revolutionary departure from traditional Marxist theory. According to Marx, capitalism will collapse because the workers will revolt. There will be class struggle, and the people will overthrow capitalism. Mason's idea is altogether different. For Mason, capitalism's inevitable demise is beginning not because of class struggle or revolt, but because of capitalism's own internal logic, and the inability to change or alter that logic. The two most important factors in its demise are digitalized abundance and globalized limitations.

How Digitalization Comes From Capitalism and Will Kill It, Too

Digitalization is inevitable under capitalism because capitalist logic seeks to drive down costs to expand margins. Contemporary business is digitalizing *everything*—business operations, books, music, movies, work, the Internet of Things, driverless cars, and working robots. Whether the products are completely digital or simply include a growing digital component, digitalization reduces operating costs and the cost of production, which results in dramatic improvements in overall profitability. Eventually, the marginal cost of production is zero. To a capitalist business person, what could be better than zero cost of production? That is why they are all digitalizing their businesses.

To understand the argument on digitalization, Mason considers the e-book. An author writes a book, and then posts it for sale on the internet. While there is cost in creating the original text, as a digital product there is no additional cost to selling the book. Whether one person or a million people download the book, the additional cost to that author/publisher is zero per unit.

In a non-digital book, the same cannot be said. Real books have a unit cost of production that incorporates printing and binding. Real production costs are important because they provide a floor on the price of the book—no publisher would sell the book below the cost of production, and because there is such a cost, prices can never go to zero.

So, why does this matter? In order to function, capitalism requires markets. Despite the "free market fundamentalism" of neoliberalism, which claims that markets can solve everything, markets actually do only one thing effectively—they establish prices in the short term based on the ratio of supply to demand. With digitalized products, however, supply is essentially infinite. No matter the level of demand, it won't affect the scarcity of the product, and therefore will not affect the price. The supply/demand ratio, which determines price, is rendered meaningless. Because there is zero marginal cost of production, there is no floor to keep prices above zero either. Both factors will drive prices of digital products to zero. As that happens, the supply and demand ratio breaks down completely, and the pricing mechanism in markets, on which capitalism depends, cannot function.

Globalized Limits

Just as capitalist logic drives down costs, capitalism is the engine behind globalization—it is robust and inevitable, a veritable juggernaut. Globalization did not derive from a hidden desire for capitalist conquest; rather, globalization is required by the logic of capitalism itself. As Mason explains, economists have always known that as capitalism develops, it periodically comes to a crisis of profitability. Innovations lead to new products, the products are sold at a premium until competition enters the market, and then competition begins to commoditize the products and profits begin to fall. As profits fall, capitalism hits a crisis point which can only be solved by accessing new markets. One response is through innovation to meet new needs, and the other is to physically enter new geographic markets. Starting in the 16th century, capitalism drove exploration and conquest primarily to open new markets, a process that has continued to this day.

Mason makes an interesting point: in this globalized world in which we now live, which new markets remain to be conquered? Globalization means that capitalism is everywhere, and untouched indigenous societies no longer exist. So, as profits fall, which they inevitably do in capitalism, the classic response to expand into new markets is no longer an option. Capitalism as a system has nowhere to go; it will not be able to expand into new markets to restore profitability. As Mason points out, these geographic limitations bring 500 years of capitalist expansion to an abrupt halt. If profits can't be resurrected, capitalism is over.

Instantly Global

A third dynamic, which Mason misses, is crucial: while non-digital products in traditional capitalism "go global" over time, digital products are instantly global. In traditional capitalism, the companies marketing goods and services build distribution infrastructure and other mechanisms needed to get to market—and to obtain what is needed to create the products. Individual companies create these classic distribution channels and supply chains, and tend to globalize them over time.

Digital products are completely different—they are immediately global in both the supply chain and distribution. In the digital world, there is only one market, and it is a global market. Access to that market will equate with capitalistic development as more people gain access to the internet. Nonetheless, there are no supply chains and no distribution channels to create. Authors, musicians, and movie makers have experienced this first hand—when a song or book is published, it is available immediately and everywhere.

Digitalization drives prices toward zero, and it accesses all markets all the time. Market expansion as a strategy to support profits and perpetuate capitalism is no longer available because capitalism has made the world into a single, universal market.

The result is a perfect storm in which capitalism creates the conditions for its own demise:

- Digital products and services create an abundance that makes it impossible for markets to price those goods and services
- Prices and margins fall toward zero
- Profits cannot be reinvigorated through market expansion

Under these conditions, capitalism cannot function because it cannot price its constituent activities. What is the value of work to create a product whose price is zero? How does a capitalist business leader justify an investment if the product cannot generate a return? What price would one pay to accumulate capital that cannot generate a profit? Indeed, what does money even mean?

Mason's view is not the opinion of a moralizing critic, but rather, it is a cool-headed analysis of the system itself. It opens many intriguing questions: What if he is right? What will replace capitalism? How will the world look when capitalism cannot function effectively anymore and loses its ideological hegemony? Mason makes an attempt to answer these questions, and although his approach is instructive, it is ultimately unsatisfactory. That is why I explore these questions in detail in the following essays.

The Supposed Guide to Our Future

While Mason provides an intriguing insight into the driving forces behind an inevitable postcapitalism, his descriptions of the outcome fall into a traditional perspective of the political left. Mason's analysis draws upon leading capitalist system thinkers like Peter Drucker and Adam Smith, as well as its most prominent critics and analysts, including Nikolai Kondratieff and of course, Karl Marx. While that balanced and bifurcated view enables his insightful historical analysis, it may also have limited his view of the future possibilities. If his analysis is correct, this bifurcation itself will become meaningless and irrelevant because the question is not where we will end up on the left-right spectrum, but rather, how does the new spectrum that will replace the left-right view give meaning and perspective in this new postcapitalist world?

Mason provides five principles for managing the changes to the postcapitalist future:

- Understand the limitations of human willpower in the face of a complex and fragile system
- Design the transition for ecological sustainability
- The transition will be a human transition—it goes well beyond economics
- Attack the problem from all angles, especially using networks
- Maximize the power of information

One can already see a prescribed outcome in these principles. These so-called principles are worth investigating, but they presuppose an ability to control and prescribe without giving a reason to believe that they will be any more effective than the capitalists will be at controlling and prescribing their own direction. Mason goes on to be quite explicit in describing that:

> *"The top level aims of a postcapitalist project should be to:*
>
> 1) *Rapidly reduce carbon emissions so that the world has warmed by only two degrees Celsius by 2050, prevent an energy crisis and mitigate the chaos caused by climate events.*
>
> 2) *Stabilize the finance system between now and 2050 by socializing it, so that ageing populations, climate change and the debt overhang do not combine to detonate a new boom-bust cycle and destroy the world economy.*
>
> 3) *Deliver high levels of material prosperity and wellbeing to the majority of people, primarily by prioritizing information-rich technologies towards solving major social challenges, such as ill health, welfare dependency, sexual exploitation and poor education.*
>
> 4) *Gear technology towards the reduction of necessary work to promote the rapid transition towards an automated economy. Eventually, work becomes voluntary, basic commodities and public services are free, and economic management becomes primarily an issue of energy and resources, not capital and labour."*[41]

Although these aims may be admirable for a social political program, they are disappointing because there is nothing inevitable about these outcomes. There is nothing in the fact of digitalization, for example, that links directly or inevitably to the global warming target of two degrees Celsius. From the standpoint of his argument on the inevitability of postcapitalism, that target is completely arbitrary. Of course, two degrees Celsius has been the long-held standard of the scientific community, and there is likely extensive merit to that target, but it is not endemic to the more poignant and significant economic arguments Mason has made.

In other words, Mason argues that as capitalism meets its own demise, there is an opportunity to create a new system. He argues that we can avoid the mistakes of past attempts at central planning, and should therefore embark on a "postcapitalist project" of planning meant to accomplish laudable goals. Indeed, most postcapitalist thinkers see the emergence of postcapitalism as a golden opportunity for the political left. This opportunistic perspective, however, mirrors what Naomi Klein dubbed "disaster capitalism," albeit from the other end of the spectrum.[42] Rather than Milton Friedman's right wing ideologues pouncing on a disaster to remake a society as Klein documented, most postcapitalists seem to see the collapse of capitalism as their turn. They hope to create their own version of a socioeconomic experiment. This hope is not only misplaced, but also damaging to the rise of a truly postcapitalist era.

The problem is that Mason's view is steeped in the status quo. Postcapitalism, if it is to be real, will also bring about new principles and social alignments yet to be imagined. Contrary to the postcapitalist rhetoric, usurpation by Marxist or leftist ideologies will hail not a victory of postcapitalism, but rather its failure. Marxist and leftist ideologies can only exist where capitalism exists because they need it to oppose. Hence, leftist ideological victory would demonstrate that capitalism is still defining the playing field. When capitalism dissipates, there will be no left and no Marxism, and from an ideational standpoint, only the elimination of all capitalist ideologies will signal a truly new era.

Postcapitalism will not be a shift to the left; it will be a new system based on a different logic. The move from feudalism to capitalism was a qualitative change in systemic logic reflected in new principles, legal structures, and new political alignments, not merely a swing to the other end of a pre-existing spectrum.

Postcapitalists should not establish planned outcomes. Instead, they should be looking to define that new, intrinsic logic and the relevant societal institutions and principles needed to guide the postcapitalist future. Hence, a more compelling argument than Mason's would focus on how to change that underlying logic. After all, the original argument presupposes that the logic of capitalism is leading to this postcapitalist world in what could be a very dramatic, possibly catastrophic collapse. Rather than a leftist political project meant to bend the economic system to its will, a truly radical approach imagines the new principles of a new economic system.

It might be useful to propose some slightly different questions:

- If in the past capitalism survived based on a logic that creates, invades, and dominates new markets, what new logic will arise so that such creation, invasion, and domination is not required for the economic system to work?
- Because is it unlikely to happen all at once, what are the opportunities for adding value within the capitalist system and for setting up alternatives to that system as capitalism wanes? When and where should we be ready to act?
- As postcapitalism emerges, what are the likely impacts on the international monetary system—what would happen to central banks and global financial markets?
- What *economic* opportunities should be engaged to help establish beachheads and alternatives to meeting the very real economic needs of people in a world where capitalism begins to fail, climate is changing rapidly, and all the old rules are falling apart?
- How will capitalism and business respond in the short and intermediate term? What role will business have?

For example, Mason raises the notion of universal basic income (UBI) in which everyone is given enough monthly income to live on. He, like many other advocates of UBI, poses this as an idea to free labor and overthrow capitalism. Certainly, it would require major changes in the system.

Less obvious, however, is that UBI may become the response to capitalism's most basic need in a globalized market—UBI creates a new market into which capitalism can expand. Businesses need new markets, and the suddenly empowered consumers receiving UBI become that new market. Just as digitalization, which is driven by capitalist business logic, will make markets nonfunctional due to pricing problems, UBI, which capitalism will require to survive, will undercut capitalism's exploitation of labor. However, UBI is unlikely to evolve based on ideological argument—there are far too many forces arrayed against the ideology. Rather, UBI will come into being in the service of a capitalism desperate for new markets. In other words, it will evolve out of capitalism's intrinsic logic, not as a result of a Marxist revolution—a realization that dramatically increases the possibility of UBI occurring.

UBI developing because capitalist elites need it is one example of underlying logic leading to a postcapitalist world. We need to go beyond advocacy and toward understanding the new logic. Postcapitalism will not be delineated by different policies, but by new logic.

I cannot thank Mason enough for his cogent economic history and analysis. Moving forward, we need imagination, but not about policies and outcomes. We need to imagine this new economic logic because the world we live in was not created by greedy people, but by people employed to live out a capitalistic logic that was given to them. This new logic is where I, others, and hopefully Mason himself will turn next, with the hope of giving new generations a different experience of their time on this earth.

The Folly of Demands: An Argument with Inventing the Future

By Nick Srnicek and Alex Williams

After a lifetime of reading hundreds of books criticizing the status quo from the standpoint of environmental problems, social justice, equal rights, and similar progressive perspectives, I continually find myself confounded by a troubling question: why is it that when so many good people know so many smart and wise things, the world just keeps getting worse? Whether it is authors with insights like Wendell Berry, Jerry Mander, Bill McKibben, and Frances Moore Lappe, or protest actions like Occupy, Black Lives Matter, and fossil fuel divestiture, or trends like organic food, local food, and even local currencies, great insights and tons of work and energy are put forth by great people, but the world keeps getting worse, not better. Income inequality is worse. Mass incarceration is worse. Catastrophic climate collapse looms, and carbon levels are getting worse. What is going on when so many people care, many of them take action, and yet the march of the system continues unabated and all the problems just keep getting worse?

Inventing the Future, by Nick Srnicek and Alex Williams provides the answer. The world is getting worse because the left is too narrow, parochial, and limited in its demands. If we are to invent a new future, they say, we must invigorate demands and class struggle to achieve a postcapitalist society. Their critique of leftist political action of the past is cogent and insightful, but if we accept their direction in how to shape the postcapitalist future, we are likely to miss this unique opportunity to overthrow capitalism and replace it with a system altogether different.

The authors' thesis in the beginning of the book amounts to a critique not only of strategy and tactics, but of the actual thought process that progressives use to frame their view of the world. Srnicek and Williams see that the old slogan "think globally, act locally," has destroyed the progressive left's intellectual and political power. For example, the problem is not the invasion of extractive mining and oil production in a beautiful place like Equador, nor is it the anti-labor policies of Tory governments in the UK. The problem is not that the minimum wage is too low, or that there are too many people in prison. No, the problem is a system that creates all those problems. While local projects like the Keystone pipeline, off-shore drilling, massive dams, or local developments should be challenged, even a stream of wins by what Naomi Klein calls "Blockadia" will not change the system. It simply pushes the capitalist forces fighting for those projects to other locations until circumstances become more amenable, and then they return to do the project originally envisioned.

The problem the authors accurately identify is this: you cannot challenge and overturn a global scale system responsible for changing the climate of every place on the globe with even the most successful local action. "Folk politics," which is local in its arena and horizontal in its structure, cannot win against a globalized hierarchical system like neoliberal capitalism. Some people may protest that statement, but indigenous cultures have been losing that exact same battle for centuries now—all across North and south America, throughout Africa, in remote villages in Europe, and elsewhere. Successes, such as they are, are measured in isolated battles; for progressives and social justice advocates, it has been one very long war, and year after year, the war is being lost.

Part of the challenge is that these folk politics are a very natural, intuitive response to the problem as we see it. Here is how Srnicek and Williams describe it:

> *"Against the abstraction and inhumanity of capitalism, folk politics aims to bring politics down to the 'human scale' by emphasising temporal, spatial and conceptual immediacy. At its heart, folk politics is the guiding intuition that immediacy is always better and often more authentic, with the corollary being a deep suspicion of abstraction and mediation. In terms of temporal immediacy, contemporary folk politics typically remains reactive (responding to actions initiated by corporations and governments, rather than initiating actions); ignores long-term strategic goals in favour of tactics (mobilizing around single-issue politics or emphasising process); prefers practices that are often inherently fleeting (such as occupations and temporary autonomous zones); chooses the familiarities of the past over the unknowns of the future (for instance, the repeated dreams of a return to 'good' Keynesian capitalism); and expresses itself as a*

> *predilection for the voluntarist and spontaneous over the institutional (as in the romanticisation of rioting and insurrection)."[43]*

Most progressives with reasonable self-awareness will admit these preferences and tendencies. Yet, with that paragraph, the authors capture the essence of one answer to my question. Why is the world getting worse? *Because resistance has remained local and parochial, and that has made it utterly ineffective.* Worse, this has happened because of the progressive opposition's own decisions—we have gutted our own power by focusing on local folk politics and refusing the burdens of theoretical frameworks and comprehensive ideology. In a very real sense, progressives have not lost the war, they have given it away!

As the left prepares to tackle the challenges of the future, these lessons should go with us. Small may be beautiful, but it's not very effective at transforming global capitalism. Although the authors sound a clarion bell on this point, they fail to see how their own prescription for the future is just as problematic. Leaving behind folk politics is crucial, but if the strategy is to immerse the left in a capitalist left-right dualism, the outcome will be no different than if folk politics remained the dominant leftist paradigm. Capitalism would simply endure. And when capitalism endures, no change is meaningful.

The second half of *Inventing the Future* argues for a leftist political approach to the economy, the kind of strategy that would be required, and steps to take toward that specific outcome. The outcome is based on *"the realisation of four minimal demands:*

1. *Full automation*
2. *The reduction of the working week*
3. *The provision of a basic income*
4. *The diminishment of the work ethic"[44]*

In other words, their vision of postcapitalism is a post-work world for everyone—that is, a world in which work is no longer required to make a living and earn your subsistence.

Two things should be said about this program and vision. First, the authors present a comprehensive model for leading political change whose goal is a bigger achievement than this protest or that blockade. The model they follow, strangely enough, is the multi-decade rise and development of neoliberal ideology. The neoliberal project started in the 1930s with ideas and inspiration from Leo Strauss and Friedrich Hayek of the Austrian School of Economics, and was taken up at the University of Chicago by Milton Friedman and others in the 1950s. In the 1960s, these intellectual forces began think tanks, published papers and articles, and changed the whole notion of "common sense." After all, nearly everyone agrees that:

- Markets are good, or at least a fact of life
- Free trade creates growth
- Minimum wage stifles employment
- Inflation should be 2 percent
- Everyone should have a job

Even if you don't personally agree with one or more of these, the ubiquitous nature of these ideas constitutes a "common sense." We call it "reality," but we only think of this as reality because of a concerted effort to make it so. It is a *neoliberal* common sense.

If neoliberalism needed a multi-decade program to become the dominant hegemonic ideology of our day, the same will be required for a postcapitalist ideology to come to the fore as well. Specifically, people are needed to:

- Develop new ideas and promulgate them until they become the "common sense" of the era.
- Do the political work, the religious work, and the organizing work.
- Develop institutions that support the ideology, or sometimes infiltrate those institutions that will do it.

The vision is big, bold, theoretical, and comprehensive. It would never settle for any specific, parochial, or local interest. It would push beyond local food, beyond a project blockade, and beyond a protest action. The target is systemic change which will affect everyone.

Second, although this vision is bold and comprehensive, it is inadequate. The size and scope are sound from the standpoint of systemic change to the postcapitalist economy. But capitalism is more than just an economic system—it is an ideology, an idea framework for understanding the world. If one accepts that notion, then why should we think it adequate to create a vision for change that is completely immersed in the capitalist ideological framework? An argument based on a left-right political economic alignment is doomed to find itself immersed in the same battles lost in the past. Here are some examples of how the authors frame this discussion:

- *"Labour organisations have traditionally been significant forces of social transformation, but today they find themselves on the back foot. At the same time, deeply entrenched habits and inflexible—if not outright corrupt—union leaderships have made the revitalisation of these organisations an uphill battle. Yet they remain indispensable to the transformation of capitalism, and any effort to imagine a new union structure must learn lessons from both the failures of older models and the changing economic conditions facing them today."*[45]
- *"A strategy may indicate the broad direction to take, but it still leaves open the question of what forces exist to carry it out. Any strategy requires an active social force, mobilised into a collective formation, acting upon the world. But while putting counter-hegemonic strategy into practice will require the use of power, the left has been both overwhelmed by and systematically rendered averse to the use of power."*[46]
- *"A post-work world will not emerge out of the benevolence of capitalists, the inevitable tendencies of the economy or the necessity of crisis. [...] the power of the left—broadly construed—needs to be rebuilt before a post-work society can become a meaningful strategic option."*[47]

All of these quotations harken to the rhetoric of leftist politics and proletariat revolt, thereby revealing that the perspective is ensconced in the traditional, capitalist left-right duality. Recognizing in some ways that these may not fit the current circumstances, the authors still ask a question from within that same paradigm, "Who, then, can be the transformative subject today?" and then they answer: "Despite the growing size of the surplus population and common immiseration of the proletariat, we must accept that no answer readily presents itself."[48]

The fact of that answer should be the indicator that we need a new way of thinking. Because of the left-right framework, a transformative subject is needed, and there is none. The left-right ideology assumes an exploited class will be the catalyst, or even the driving force of change. It assumes they will disrupt the system. The problem, however, is that the change is happening all around us anyway—even without this transformative subject. Technology is rapidly moving toward full automation because it is in the interests of business to do so. Universal basic income is gaining attention in wider and wider circles beyond the Marxist theorists—not because they are winning, but because capitalists are going to need such an income to further expand their markets. The system is gradually completely disrupting itself. Disruption will not be driven by transformative subjects, nor will it be unique. Disruptions will be ubiquitous. The so-called post-work world is developing along all these dimensions, but there is no transformative subject driving it. These are not the inevitable tendencies of the economy, but rather the driven self-interest of the capitalists themselves that are creating it and forcing society toward a postcapitalist world.

For this reason, the left-right framework will distort the common view of reality. The folk politics of the left, rather than being a failed strategy, is a signifier of the decline of this whole way of thinking, just as climate change is a signifier that the free market fundamentalist view of capitalism is also in decline. Neither can sustain themselves. Rather than a resurgent left, the grand theoretical framework needed now should heed the call to thought, theory, ideological scope, and transformed consciousness. We need to perceive differently what is normal, real, and true. We need a new common sense—not an old one dusted off and perked up for a new go. Struggles against capitalism have failed ever since the beginning of capitalism, and there is no reason to believe that a new struggle will work any better.

A new paradigm shift might come from realizations that challenge us in today's truly collective problems—catastrophic climate change, overpopulation, dwindling water resources. No one is getting out alone. It would surprise left-right thinkers to realize that big business has been planning for the impact of climate change since the late 1990s, at least. It would surprise left-right thinkers to know that across the business world, investors are trying to figure out solutions to water problems. The left-right framework assumes motivations on the capitalist right that are often not true, and therefore opportunities for solutions are lost.

If we truly believe there is a postcapitalist world coming, what's needed is not a leftist politics way of thinking, but a third way that encompasses a completely new framework for understanding not only our economics, but also our politics. The assertion of either side of a dualistic framework necessarily draws out and creates the opposite side of the framework. If the reformers stay in a leftist position, they will require the presence and sustenance of an oppositional right. They will remain locked in a struggle for scarce resources and rare power.

Srnicek and Williams' book moves the postcapitalist conversation forward, but it needs to keep moving. Their criticisms of the left are essential, and the vision of strategy and structure provide an open space for intellectual and political imagination. The next step in this ongoing conversation is to change the *content* of the argument. We must go beyond the staid limits of left-right capitalism and into a new worldview completely separate from that paradigm. We will know we are there when the old paradigm no longer makes any sense.

Epilogue

The essays in this book explore the possibilities of postcapitalism. They are, as the title suggests, speculative in nature. They are meant to initiate a dialog. The digital disruption to capitalism creates a unique opportunity to shape the future, and that shaping begins with ideas. What can we imagine it to be? How can we prosper in it? What will we leave behind?

The next books in this series include the following working titles:

❑ *Disrupting Capitalism: The End of the Great Mechanism and the Forces Shaping the Future*
❑ *What Is Postcapitalism? A Vision for the Postcapitalist Future*
❑ *Postcapitalist Consciousness*

These books will continue this dialog. As the books develop, many ideas appear in Intertwine: Mind * Heart * World, which is my author newsletter that includes articles, blog posts, and poems every week. <u>Please join it here</u>.

There is plenty of room for additional voices, ideas, and explorations. Please contact me if you would like to join the conversation. Write to postcapfuture@signorellli.biz. The future is going to be very different. The essays you have just read explore many possibilities, but there are many more. Let's keep the ideas alive. We are, after all, *guiding the end of capitalism and shaping what comes next.*

Works by Anthony Signorelli

On Postcapitalism
The Postcapitalism Manifesto
Speculations on Postcapitalism (print version)

For Hungry Minds…
Subscribe to **Intertwine: Mind * Heart * World**. Immediate access to blog posts, poems, tools, and special offers. Click here to sign up!
Don't miss out!

More Nonfiction
Call to Liberty: Bridging the Divide Between Liberals and Conservatives, 2006, Scarletta Press
Rooster Crows at Light from the Bombing: Poems and Essays on the Gulf War, (ed. with Paul MacAdam), 1993, Inroads Press

Notes

The Coming Collapse of Capitalism

[1] Klein, Naomi. 2015. *This Changes Everything: Capitalism vs. The Climate*. New York: Simon & Schuster.

[2] Mason 2016.

[3] Klein 2015, 224.

[4] Klein 2015, 224.

[5] Mason 2016, 238-239.

[6] Mason 2016, 239.

[7] Mason 2016, 239-240.

[8] Mason 2016, 240.

[9] Ledak, Paul. 2015. "How much more computing power does an iPhone 6 have than Apollo 11?" *Quora*. January 8. https://www.quora.com/How-much-more-computing-power-does-an-iPhone-6-have-than-Apollo-11-What-is-another-modern-object-I-can-relate-the-same-computing-power-to.

[10] Mason 2016, 238.

[11] Turkle, Sherry. "The Robotic Moment: Who Do We Become When We Talk To Machines?" Lecture, Aspen Ideas Festival, Aspen, CO. June 30, 2015.

[12] Hayek, F.A., *The Road to Serfdom* (New York: Routledge, 1994), 85.

[13] Tawney, R.H. 2015. *Religion And The Rise Of Capitalism*. 3rd ed. New York: Verso.

Why Thought Matters: Paving the Road to Transition

[14] Signorelli, Anthony. 2006. *Call to Liberty: Bridging the Divide Between Liberals and Conservatives*. Minneapolis, MN: Scarletta Press.

[15] Srnicek and Williams 2015.

[16] Reagan, Ronald. "Inaugural Address." Speech, Washington DC, January 20, 1981. The American Presidency Project. http://www.presidency.ucsb.edu/ws/?pid=43130.

[17] Microsoft. "Wu Feng: Accelerating Cancer Research." February 2015. YouTube video, 1:01-1:12. https://www.youtube.com/watch?v=72w8gKJXgl4.

[18] Otte, Sander, interview by Ira Flatow. 2016. "Storing Digital Data With an 'Atomic Abacus'." *Science Friday*, 7:50-8:05. NPR. July 22.

[19] Otte 2016, 8:45-8:54.

What About the Real Economy?

[20] Stern, Andy. 2016. *Raising the Floor: How a Universal Basic Income Can Renew Our Economy and Rebuild the American Dream*. New York: PublicAffairs, 54.

Seats of Value in the Postcapitalist Economy: An Actual Guide to the Future

[21] Tawney 2015, 23.

Abundant Digital Food

[22] Memphis Meats. "Memphis Meats, Cultured Meat Company Profiled In Today's Wall Street Journal, Makes Global Debut." February 1, 2016. Web. http://www.memphismeats.com/press-releases/.

[23] Leber, Jessica. 2016. "These Meatballs Are Made Of Beef—But It Didn't Come From A Cow." *Co.Esist*. February 5. https://www.fastcoexist.com/3056325/these-meatballs-are-made-of-beef-but-it-didnt-come-from-a-cow.

[24] Prokopanko, James. *The Mosaic Company*. First Tuesday Luncheon, University of Minnesota, Minneapolis, MN. April 5, 2016.

[25] Frase, Peter. 2016. *Four Futures: Life After Capitalism*. New York: Verso.

Problems and Opportunities with the Universal Basic Income Dream

[26] Matthews, Chris. 2016. "Comrade Bill Gross Says the Federal Reserve Should Pay Your Rent." *Fortune*. May 5. http://www.fortune.com/2016/05/05/bill-gross-universal-income/.

[27] Stern 2016, 201.

[28] Bain, Marc. 2016. "Robots are set to take the jobs of millions of Asian workers in the coming years." *Quartz*. July 8. http://www.qz.com/727102/robots-are-set-to-take-the-jobs-of-millions-of-asian-workers-in-the-coming-years/.

[29] Popper, Nathaniel. 2016. "The Robots Are Coming for Wall Street." *The New York Times Magazine*. February 25. http://www.nytimes.com/2016/02/28/magazine/the-robots-are-coming-for-wall-street.html?_r=0.

[30] Davies, Alex. 2016. "Uber's Self-Driving Truck Makes Its First Delivery: 50,000 Beers." *Wired*. October 25. https://www.wired.com/2016/10/ubers-self-driving-truck-makes-first-delivery-50000-beers/.

[31] Proctor, Bernadette D., Jessica L. Semega, and Melissa A. Kollar. 2016. "Income and Poverty in the United States: 2015." *US Census Bureau, Current Population Reports*, 5. https://www.census.gov/content/dam/Census/library/publications/2016/demo/p60-256.pdf.

[32] Stern 2016, 212-214.

[33] Heffter, Emily. 2014. "US Renters Spent $441 Billion on Rent in 2014." *Zillow Porchlight*. December 30. http://www.zillow.com/blog/us-renters-spent-441-billion-2014-167117/.
[34] Mason 2016, 13.

Toward a Postcapitalist Plan for Trade and Distribution

[35] France-Presse, Agence. 2016. "Reboot: Adidas to make shoes in Germany again—but using robots." *The Guardian*. May 24. https://www.theguardian.com/world/2016/may/25/adidas-to-sell-robot-made-shoes-from-2017.
[36] Hoskins, Tansy. 2016. "Robot factories could threaten jobs of millions of garment workers." *The Guardian*. July 16. https://www.theguardian.com/sustainable-business/2016/jul/16/robot-factories-threaten-jobs-millions-garment-workers-south-east-asia-women.

Postcapitalism, Networks, and the New Post-State World

[37] SparkNotes Editors. 2005. *SparkNote on Leonardo da Vinci*. http://www.sparknotes.com/biography/davinci/.

What Will Corporations Do in a Post-Capitalist World?

[38] Mason 2016.
[39] Mander, Jerry. 1992. *In the Absence of the Sacred: The Failure of Technology and the Survival of the Indian Nations*. San Francisco, CA: Sierra Club Books, 126.
[40] Mander, Jerry. 2013. *The Capitalism Papers: Fatal Flaws of an Obsolete System*. Berkeley, CA: Counterpoint.

Arguments with Postcapitalism: *A Guide to Our Future*, by Paul Mason

[41] Mason, Paul. 2016. *Postcapitalism: A Guide to Our* Future. New York: Farrar, Straus and Giroux, 269-270.
[42] Klein, Naomi. 2007. *The Shock Doctrine: The Rise of Disaster* Capitalism. London: Picador.

The Folly of Demands: An Argument with *Inventing the Future*

[43] Srnicek, Nick, and Alex Williams. 2015. *Inventing the Future: Postcapitalism and a World Without Work*. New York: Verso, 10.

---

[44] Srnicek and Williams 2015, 127.
[45] Srnicek and Williams 2015, 166.
[46] Srnicek and Williams 2015, 155.
[47] Srnicek and Williams 2015, 174.
[48] Srnicek and Williams 2015, 158.